Contents

Editorial

As the petulant UK floats away from the continent and out into the ocean, we welcome you to our North Atlantic Drift edition. Sometimes art can be necessarily prescient. When we started commissioning work for this edition of *Gutter* in late 2015, we had no idea of the political insanity that would envelop our islands shortly before we went to press.

Since it began in 2009, this magazine has always had a commitment to internationalism at its core. This is not borne out of some vague idealism, but of a firm belief in the ability of words and ideas to join people in conversation and collaboration much more than they can ever foster difference and division. It is about the existence, not ownership, of the creative milieu. We also have shown dedication to the imperfect art of publishing work in translation, as an opaque window into the thoughts and desires of other cultures. For this reason, previous issues of *Gutter* have featured work from writers with native idioms including Arabic, German, Spanish, Chinese, French, Italian, Turkish, Polish and many others.

For this issue we decided to reach out across the Atlantic to writers from Canada and Iceland, two countries that have much in common with Scotland in terms of history, landscape and culture. Their work also reminds us that we still live in a world where ICBMs point across the ocean, primed for a minutes-long journey of destruction where once longboats took days. We are delighted to include a story by acclaimed Icelandic writer Auður Jónsdóttir that explores the very internationalism and (in)tolerance that has dominated our streets and headlines these last few months. For poetry, we have two pieces of work by Valgerður Þóroddsdóttir, selected from her new chapbook.

During a workshop last year, we met up with Canadian poets from the Shaken & Stirred collective, and we are pleased to include work by Ian Burgham, Catherine Graham, Steven Heighton and Jeanette Lynes. The poems from *SUND* by Angela Rawlings complete the Icelandic-Canadian connection, referencing back to Old Norse via weapons of mass destruction.

Closer to home, the trans-Atlantic theme continues with Shetlanders Mallachy Tallack (author of *Sixty Degrees North*) and Christie Williamson, who makes a welcome return to the magazine. We are particularly grateful to include a piece from the brilliant James Kelman, whose early writing was informed by his experiences as a young man in the USA, and whose work still burns with the linguistic intensity of his American realist progenitors and his post-colonial peers. This is James's first appearance here and we are chuffed to have him. James's work was among the first contemporary Scottish fiction encountered by a certain member of the *Gutter* editorial team and, while he'll probably hate us for saying so, it is partly due to his inspiration that this mag exists.

We (possibly foolishly) mentioned the North Atlantic theme on our website some months ago and we'd like to thank our submitters for all the stories about ice, cod and polar bears... Among those we picked are two tectonic short stories that take place along the North Atlantic Ridge: 'Asibikaashi' by RA Davis and 'The Offset and The Calving' by Ryan Vance, plus Brian Docherty's reflections on the thoughts of the walrus and Jane Goldman's concrete 'Oor Moby: Möbius'. There are related pieces on place and language from Alec Finlay (also making his début in *Gutter*, welcome), Carol McKay, Arun Sood, William Bonar and Roseanne Watt. Off theme, there is the usual smörgåsbord of words and punctuation to provoke and enlighten the weary reader.

Two recent events around the centennial of the Battle of the Somme, gave us pause to reflect on our potential futures in or out of the European Union. The first, being stuck in traffic behind an orange march along Dumbarton Road, Glasgow, was a portent of the UKIP-future that the Brexit referendum result has propelled us towards: impotent, hateful, unable to move forward, lodged (pardon the pun) behind a pompous little pelleton of red-white-and-blue, bowler-hatted bile that has got stuck in the gullet of Britain. The second was Jeremy Deller's 'human memorial' performance art piece We're Here Because We're Here, in which small groups of ordinary working citizens dressed in World War One army uniforms congregated publicly on trains, in railway stations, shopping centres, car parks and outside public buildings at 8am on the morning of the battle's anniversary. In simultaneous, silent, unsentimental, unannounced gatherings, the participants mingled silently among commuters or quietly sang an old song from the trenches to the tune of Auld Lang Syne. Each participant represented a person who lost their life on that first day of industrial slaughter, and each silently gave out a calling card with the victim's personal details to any passersby who enquired. This was a true people's memorial, eschewing the ugly certainties of the orangemen, UKIP or the Tory party. It was also a timely reminder of the folly and horror that follows when ordinary people allow themselves swept up in the jingoism of their masters – as John Maclean said in Glasgow one hundred years ago, 'a bayonet is a weapon with a working man at either end.'

Europe today faces different but related horrors: there are strong echoes of 1916 in the bellicose utterances of the Little Englanders (and indeed, some Little Scotlanders), the treatment of foreigners in our country and an imperialist proxy war in Syria – the consequences of which are leaching steadily into Europe. It is increasingly clear that the Tory party has committed an act of national vandalism in an attempt to settle an Eton tiff, but it is vital that those who believe in internationalism fight to minimise the impact of their democratic idiocy.

Why does this matter? If we are such true internationalists, then surely we transcend institutions like the EU? Is it not simply a free trade cabal? As writers, editors and artists, our answer is pragmatic and fourfold: one, the EU treaty allows us unparalleled freedom of movement to take our work to new audiences across its 27 countries and beyond, it allows us to sell this magazine, free of tariffs, anywhere from Lisbon to Latvia; two, its institutions and legal frameworks protect our right to free expression in a way that many would seek to erode; three, the European project provides huge opportunity for creative interchange between nations and cultures, to say nothing of people (think of all the beautiful romances that free movement has enabled); four, the EU helps to support the arts on a scale that would be unaffordable to small nations acting alone. This support ranges from funding to help writers develop careers, to formal networks that enable writers to engage with new audiences.

We are not naïve, the EU is not perfect. Its bureaucrats are aloof, its workings inefficient and in need of reform, it has proved unable or unwilling to support the refugees fleeing to its shores. And where it has provided deprived communities in England and Scotland with billions of pounds in grant assistance, it has clearly failed to communicate its utility to many of those who benefited and who voted to Leave. Much of the blame there lies at the door of politicians and the mainstream media for ignoring these people for decades, then failing to advocate the benefits of continued membership and allowing the anti-immigration narrative to dominate the referendum debate. But leaving the EU is not the answer. Leaving allows the dark forces of neoconservative economics and racist division to consolidate their hold on the UK, and this must be opposed.

Ah, you say, 'but you have Icelanders in this issue? Iceland is outwith the EU.' Correct, but Iceland is within the European Economic Area. It has access to free movement and trade, protections that look increasingly unlikely to be agreed during Brexit because of the right's obsession with immigration. We will therefore end up more like the Canadian writers in this issue, who have had to apply for costly work permits to attend our August launch events in Edinburgh and Glasgow.

We cannot end our thoughts on Europe without mentioning the obvious: the fact that Scotland voted overwhelmingly to remain in the EU against the overall UK result. Even more so than in 1992, 2010 or 2015, it is evident that the views of the English and Scottish electorates are poles apart, and that again the smaller partner in this Union is being pulled by its neighbour, against its will, towards a dangerous, uncertain future.

Recently, a wag at the Tory-friendly Centre for Policy Studies concluded that Scotland leaving the UK 'would entail significant economic risk'. That much is obvious, and something would need to be done to close the gap between Scotland's tax income and public expenditure. But it would be an economic risk of our choosing, supported by our European partners, as opposed to remaining in the UK as an afterthought to London with utterly no control. Beware any politician who tells you otherwise. The Centre for Policy Studies cheekily went on to suggest that we risk becoming Greece without the sunshine: 'There is a precedent for a small, romantic country, surrounded by hundreds of islands, perched on the extremity of Europe, seeking membership of the euro: Greece.' While we are flattered by the comparison to Hellenic beauty, we would argue that Scotland's public finances are considerably less 'challenging' than our Mediterranean friends, they are also more transparent, and we stand to benefit greatly - both economically and artistically - from unfettered links to Europe.

During the 2014 referendum, much was made of the economic uncertainties of Scottish independence, and if we are being honest we agree that this is where the Yes campaign was at its weakest: the currency policy in particular did not stand up to close scrutiny. Now, the situation is utterly changed: the UK economy is in deepening crisis, and whichever way Scotland turns, it is facing an uncertain future. Given our country's long previous experience of being London's fiscal whipping boy whenever the UK enters hard times, who in their right mind would wish for Scotland to remain handcuffed to an economically suicidal partner that has just leapt into the abyss? We are by no means cheerleaders for the SNP, but the Scottish Government is correct in its current approach to seek the best deal for the country in Europe. If this is not forthcoming then we also fully support the concept of a second independence referendum, and we will once again be voting Yes. In the meantime we hope that you enjoy this issue while we drift out into the North Atlantic.

Unidentified Aircraft (over Montrose)

Claire Quigley

– after the painting by Edward Baird –

This is the stillness just before.
The town lies faceted behind.
We threw a bridge across

the unreflecting river
like a living cord – still warm –
under a sky shown day for night.

Snowfall has shattered on the hills.
We are so close that you are almost
with us now, as we – still warm –

lift up our faces to the night.
Arms wide, priests
of a silent benediction:

that our bodies might leave
angels in the snow
if we should fall.

a fool's mind

Alec Finlay

I could scatter
    the clouds over
        Monadh Ruadh

blow the thistle-
    down off Tom
        Chluaran

shine every last leaf
    on the birches of
        Coire nan Craobh-bheithe

pluck you a flake
    of sharp flint
        from Blar-nan-Saighead

plait you the tale
    of a crepuscular tiger
        in Fluich Adagan

look away if you
    get a rise out
        of Clach a' Bhodaich

wrap the stone
    with new wool
        by Allt nan Cuigeal

warm the White Calf
    in the snows
        of The Brown Cow

gather the rose
    from the fold
        of Allt Fileachaidh

carry you safe
over the Water
Splash

find where hazel grow
by the fleet-water
of Allt Challa

but mending a fool's
mind's something
I cannot do

Gorse

Leonie M Dunlop

Let Scotland burn yella,
mak the gorse oor national flooer,
a blaze tearin across every terrain
it lives in: the crags, the sands, the fields.

Nae mair singin fur the thistle:
the one sang wi dour faces afore a match
when we lose.

Gie us back oor brightest bush,
once mashit fur fuel an fodder.

The one that would sing loudest
at a curry and karaoke night,
tarted up in the reek o coconut-de-cologne-cooncil-juice.
She's been through duty free, been abroad, don't you know?

Cousin o the wispy whin and kenned as furze:
We relish spying them set alight oor land
and roar away the bleak stereotype of oor hame,
makin yella enough o a flag fur us.

What the Walrus Thought

Brian Docherty

That the persistence of easterly weather
was down to malevolence, not the season,
two weeks short of winter solstice,
not to some combination of tide and wind
patterns, and certainly not to theories
about climate change or global warming.

The walrus had never seen a scientist
close up, although it had once taken
umbrage at David Attenborough's
cameraman, but it had learned from
its mother that humans were bad luck.
It knew to avoid humans, boats and orcas.

Apart from those, it could do whatever
it pleased to anything that came its way,
even polar bears; weather was another
matter, it had enough sense and memory
to expect and recognise patterns, but not
enough for anything like religious belief.

If elephants, dolphins, or whales enjoy
a religious experience, this must be severely
tested by what humans do to the world
they are obliged to share with these others.
The walrus does not waste time with this,
it just goes its surly way in the world.

It has three aims in its world, no plan,
no objectives, just a settled conviction
that things could be better, that someone
or something just out of sight, maybe you,
maybe David Attenborough, but more than
wind and weather, has put it in this position.

Headliners 1 & 2 & 3

James McGonigal

Here they come, all the little things –
jubilant Sundays, a tidal timetable,
a pair of thrawn dualists consuming

roast rat and terrapin. Either or
neither. Tomorrow the gypsy plague
will be right back

emancipating and enslaving.
Never quite too high a bill and
worth paying, he says she says

on the beach walking his dog.

*

On delirium days beyond the ideal
a talking corpse in corduroys
burned deep, suspended in smoke.

Organs underground were sacrificial acts,
tentacular ritualisms. Poker faces
looking for someone to blame.

She had once been queen of two
boot-shaped territories, getting nowhere
with either. Now liking it hot:

Beethoven played on a mouth organ.

*

It started with a 'No'
denying shelf life to the academics
of violence on all fronts.

Home with the fairies
the promise of blue harmonious voices
calmed everything down.

Never as free as when delicacy
skinned their uglier feelings alive,
sojourners in Moscow kept

a restless eye on signs and boundaries.

Akker

Roseanne Watt

'He who loses his language loses his world'
– Iain Crichton Smith

These days,
I think more and more
about the tongue
of some luckless ancestor

weighed down
by ess and soapstone
in a bog somewhere

(perhaps on the wast side of the island
where the heather grows thickest,
and the corbies look meanest,
where I heard all the lost things go)

and so perfectly preserved
you could even trace the taste
of her own last supper,
catch the cadence
of her last word spoken –

a word
that I can never know
even if I'd heard it said,

her language
dead now;

all akker,
absence,

like how sea-glass
bears no mindin
of the bottle, nor the liquid
which it kept, the lips
that wrapped around its neck,

the message
it once held
inside itself.

I plunder such pieces
on the slud days
when words leave me
at a loss, and all
near-hearted, present things
have sunk
into their darknesses;

in those smallest devastations
of the light,
I fear the silence
which the hills give back.

About Poetry

AP Pullan

The boy with Asperger's shows me his world of
Lego and Plasticine, that stretches to the edge of The Badlands.
Today I'm not teacher but the food boy. He can grant such things.

Five papier mâché suns, one for each of his family,
shine on rivers that run blue only at night.
Here you must watch for Measle bats and here

the jack of clubs guards from a tower of bricks as
there might be dragons.
It's just the way I see things, how things could be.

Stay if you want and listen for their sound a bit like
when you shake out a big blanket. I don't tell him about simile
but instead lay down and just listen

'Allahu akbar!' she hears shouted again as a myriad of voices giggle and shout in anticipation.

On the Way to the Writers' Conference

Auður Jónsdóttir

On the Way to the Writers' Conference

Auður Jónsdóttir

(translated by Larissa Kyzer)

The child murderer lived at home with his parents in a cosy neighborhood in the outskirts of Berlin. With a tidy garden. German flags in the flowerbeds, in amongst heady flowering trees that smelled like a bomb had dropped into a perfume factory.

Maybe he ate his breakfast outside – ripe strawberries, freshly ground coffee, freshly pressed orange juice and rolls with cheese and organic marmalade – while he toyed with thoughts of how he could torture a five-year-old boy to death.

He intrudes on her thoughts every morning, such that she doesn't realise it before she's raised her voice with her son.

'Hurry up,' she says.

'Why?' asks her son, baffled by the shrill command.

'Because I'm going to be late for a conference of European writers,' says his mother, instinctively smiling at the formality of her own words. She regularly amuses herself by answering him in such a way that the answer invites more questions. In this case, she should have known better.

'What's that?' he asks.

She regards him, his sunburnt face under a golden shock of hair that has long since grown over his eyes and dampens the curiosity that shines out from them. How shall she explain a symposium on the eternal tug of war between hate speech and freedom of speech to a five-year-old boy? Then all at once she remembers that the conference website had talked about borders and she takes pains to explain the matter: 'Writers get together at the conference to discuss how their stories can break down borders.'

'What are borders, mom?'

'Put on your shoes,' she says, 'or else I'll be late and they won't let me in.'

'But what are borders?' He stares at her so eagerly that his dark brown eyes turn black. With his lips pursed, resolved to hold his breath until she answers.

'They are lines that we create in our heads to decide where a country begins and where it ends,' she says after some deliberation.

'Lines around countries?' asks the kid, so animated that his body practically levitates when he runs to the puzzle map that hangs on the wall. She bought it for him in Sardinia the summer before and had to pay fifty euros extra at the airport to take it home to Berlin.

Now he's started to piece the puzzle together when, according to the painstaking schedule she conceived when they went to bed the night before, they should have left long before. Last night, she'd visualised quite clearly how the morning would go. And now they are both going to be too late.

'Put on your shoes, right this second!' Her voice sounded unpleasantly shrill. She wouldn't be so brusque except that her German translator had promised to treat her to a glass of champagne at lunch if she came to the conference to speak about all the words in the world.

'Is this line a border?' asks her son without batting an eye and pointing at a yellow continent that she sees right away is Africa.

'If you don't put on your shoes right now – this instant – you won't get ice cream after kindergarten!' She groans and looks at the clock.

'Daddy says you aren't allowed to bribe me.'

'I'm not bribing you. You don't even know what that means.'

'Yeah – this.'

'Anyway, your father's abroad.'

'Why?'

'Put on your shoes,' she commanded as she slipped on her tennis shoes. Then she threw on a cardigan and hustled him into a jean jacket.

'Why isn't daddy with us?'

'I've already told you that.'

He purses his lips together again, standing rigidly in the sunbeams that bathe the light room and the paintings on the wall: one German Expressionist, a few Icelandic abstract works, and a self-portrait of a kindergarten-aged child. A potted plant the size of a man seems to have gotten even bigger in the brightness and she becomes uncomfortably aware of the fine dust that lies around them from the books in the bookshelf that they bought from a Polish translator when they moved here from Reykjavík.

Berlin is blanketed in light this fresh May morning. She's dying for a coffee – her chest strains with longing for caffeine.

She can hardly wait to go speeding through the sunny and leaf-green city in a taxi with a to-go coffee in one hand and her tablet computer in the other and she lets herself dream about the day ahead, the remarks that she expects to hear and also those that have yet to surprise her.

She's heard it all before – the arguments for freedom of expression and the arguments for human rights, leveled by dissimilar groups, in various, contradictory forms – and still, still she feels like she has yet to hear something that genuinely matters. Something that no one has ever put a finger on. Perhaps she'll hear it today, but then she has to hurry. The only wise thing to do is to pick up the phone. Call a taxi. Now.

Her son forages through her dark hair to remind her of his existence. Tender when he smiles, almost paternal.

So charmingly independent that she feels her stress giving way to a longing to embrace him and give herself up to it so unreservedly that he'll forget his questions, just this once.

'Put on your shoes now, sweetheart,' she says mildly and pulls herself free from his grip.

'That's what I'm doing.'

'Then let me see you doing it!'

He obeys but she sighs. He'd ambushed her with questions since they woke up, just before eight AM. Each one leading to another. Of course she should take his father's advice: throw on some clothes and hop into a taxi with their son and let him run into the kindergarten by himself.

But she's determined to follow him on foot all the way up to the door. Even though she tries as best she can to reason with herself, reminds herself that it borders on mania to follow routines blindly. She's addicted to their mornings, the morning is a constant that nothing can disrupt.

It's just after 8:30 AM and they still have a twenty-minute walk to the kindergarten before she can hop into a taxi and have the slimmest possibility of making it to the writers' conference at the Academy of Arts next to the Brandenburg Gate on time.

In the email that confirmed her participation, it said that due to great demand, registrations would become invalid at 9:15 AM so that each seat would definitely be used. A three-year residence in Berlin had taught her that it would be foolish to ignore the fine print in an email in the Germanic world. Especially when the safety of Germany's Federal Minister for Foreign Affairs would be on the line, and the registration had to be all the more precise given his brief appearance at the conference.

Finally!

She's managed to get the boy out onto the pavement. The light breeze embraces them so affectionately that they're almost surprised to feel the day in all its aggressive freshness. She takes her son's hand and they amble down the street, past the people who are joining a long line with children and strollers in front of the Red Cross to wait for the weekly clothes distribution to begin and the cherry trees that have quickly begun to darken and turn deep red. Then next past the men's coffeehouse where a round man with gap teeth and a wet mouth once launched himself at her neck.

He'd tried to barricade the two of them in a dim room that stank of stale smoke and sour sweat and, outside of a few classroom chairs and weathered tables with heaping ashtrays, was filled with nothing but gloom. The mouth of a cave inside a pale yellow apartment building.

She had felt politeness engulfing her while he talked with his eyes glued on her and stepped furtively to a window with half-obscured windowpanes to lock her in.

Then he made as though to lock the door, fawning as he prattled on in a wheedling, confidential voice about his delinquent children and aggressively pawed at her shoulders and thighs. She didn't understand why, but she froze.

It had been one of those days when the sun had confused Berlin for Benidorm, and the soles of her shoes had warmed through. But she was frozen like ice, couldn't move at all – the only thing that occurred to her was to be sufficiently polite to the man who smelled of old instant coffee and sweat.

He had given her son chocolate when they were on the way past a few days before and now he invited her in for a coffee. She had been on her way out for a jog with her headphones in and a bit drunk on adrenaline, and was stupid enough to accept in the hope of getting a fragrant mocha in a beautiful matte silver cup and taking a seat on an exquisite Persian rug – of experiencing something that the writer in her longed for, even though the woman in her tried to resist.

The writer had won out.

Deep in her heart of hearts, she'd believed that it was only thin, young, blonde women who got into such situations – not a chubby, dark-haired woman with a lopsided nose who was over forty. A woman who on top of everything else, became him, the writer, when she wrote – the masculine persona that she had taken on right after puberty.

The woman had lain down, subservient to the writer who insisted upon getting a look at a men's coffeehouse, where women were normally not allowed to step foot. In his romantic logic, the writer imagined that the man in the coffeehouse saw himself as a multiculturally inclined, thoughtful being who was getting to share his two cents with a respectable international council of writers. But the man just saw her. A woman with such large breasts that he didn't even notice her lopsided nose.

Her curiosity had drawn her in, her fear had flung her out again like a frightened rodent when she narrowly escaped him, shoved him off of her with extraordinary effort and burst breathlessly out into the sunshine.

She walked the route that she had intended to jog, but her heart pounded as if after a marathon. It had only beat so intensely once before. That was when she'd been a teenage girl in the West Fjords in Iceland working at a fish factory and a man with the nickname 'The President' had tried to shove her into a cold storage room in a bait shack.

'The President's always so goddamned horny!' laughed the other men, and their insulated coveralls had rustled when they found him and wrested him off of her. Then they all got themselves coffee from the noisy drip machine that had once been white but had since turned brown, and she hadn't thought about it again until now.

Shame spread through her with the realisation that she'd been stupid enough to give the man an opportunity to corner her in such a way. At this age. Wise in the ways of the world. Someone who knew all that she needed to know about violence: a veteran feminist writer with a grasp on clichés. And yet, a friendly invitation for a cup of coffee was enough to take her in.

Dizzy, she picks up the pace and the coffeehouse recedes behind them as she asks, 'Do you hear all the birds?'

'Yes,' says her son looking back, 'but where's the man who gave me chocolate that one time?'

She tightens her grip on his hand. 'You're not allowed to talk to him! Bad men sometimes give people chocolate to trick them.'

'But the chocolate was good,' he protests, and she knows that he's right – she had tasted it herself, dense with nuts. A piece of a chocolate bar of the size of the ones that they have in the Duty Free, that the man had unexpectedly given the boy.

She had allowed herself to be tricked like a little kid. Like the little boy who the child murderer tricked into following him last summer. Like both of the boys who he had conjured to him in a velvety voice.

He'd taken advantage of the chaos at the beginning of that period when refugees were starting to flock to Europe in such great waves that political commentators had likened the situation to the end of modern, western political culture. The child murderer had slipped into a public office for refugees and slunk through the throng – insinuated himself between mothers who'd fallen asleep with children at their breasts and exhausted fathers who dozed while keeping a watchful eye over their families – until he finally saw a little boy sitting alone on a chair. He approached the boy, gave him a teddy bear, and led him out while his mother sat in an office filling out an application for a residence permit.

The other boy had gone missing a few weeks earlier. He had been outside alone, messing around on the playground in front of his home when the man lured him over. Both of the boys were of the same age as her son.

Every day for weeks, she and her son had walked past posters requesting information about the boys, who had lived in the neighbourhood with them. Every time they came across a poster, her son asked, 'Why haven't his mummy and daddy found him?'

Each time, her legs buckled under her.

When the murderer was finally found and the media filled with stories about the boys' cruel fates, her husband asked her not to read what the murderer had done to them. 'I felt awful for a long time after I did,' he said, looking anxiously at her and holding back tears. She took his advice and a break from the news for a while. It was full of violence anyway, she thought, of pictures of dead children who had drowned on the beaches of Europe.

The ocean full of dead children and plastic.

She still thinks about the little boy who sat and waited for his mother who had conscientiously shown up amidst the chaos of German bureaucracy. She also thinks about the other boy who breathed in the smell of grass and smiled at small animals, needing no other playmate but himself. Her legs buckled again and she scanned the area quickly, ready to protect her son from the violent men who lurk where they're least expected.

How many of them were there? Mothers in Berlin who struggle with the fixation of seeing him in front of them. That skinny, pale German who has a grandmother who brings him Easter candy in jail because he was once a five-year-old boy himself.

She thinks that she'll be free of the child murderer when she goes home to Iceland, sometimes such that she flirts with the idea of moving back home to sparsely populated

Reykjavík. But he could easily be there, too. She knows that all too well. She knows that he could be anywhere so she will obstinately follow her son all the way into the kindergarten and kiss him goodbye in the vestibule of the school office, instead of just calling a taxi and letting him run into the school himself so that she'll arrive at the conference on time. She follows him as far as she can. Emotionally says her goodbyes. Every day.

What if...

Kindergarteners are often taken to large, public parks – open and wild play areas, allowed to regrow naturally after all the bombings of World War II. Most areas are so concealed by trees and shrubbery that it's painfully easy for a person who makes a living from her imagination to envision a pale man among the trees. A man who will wave a rag doll or candy in front of her child when no one is watching.

If she now has to work much longer, it's because each time she sits down to write, his bone-white, flat face appears on the computer screen and grins triumphantly at her. Even though she tries to break up the day and hurry to a conference with writers from every continent.

She's stuck.

Reeling with fear.

She derives no merriment from the spring, can't chat with colleagues in the sun out on the terrace at the Academy of Arts.

She's become empty.

'Allahu akbar!'

She jolts out of her ice-frosted preoccupations. Her hand is clammy, she's been clinging to her son's hand.

'Allahu akbar!' she hears shouted again as a myriad of voices giggle and shout in anticipation.

'What are they doing?' asks her son, wriggling with excitement as he points to a group of schoolchildren who run shrieking around the yard in front of the primary school and whirl around a chubby, awkward boy with a dark mop of hair and glasses. He spins around in circles and shouts 'Boom!' when he tries to tag the next kid. As far as she can tell, he's pretending to be a suicide bomber. Most of the kids in this school are of Turkish, Arab, and German extraction – many of them the children of people who had to flee their homelands. They trace their roots to more countries than the writers at the conference.

'They're doing the same thing as your father and I,' she whispers thunderstruck, reminding herself of Sir David Attenborough face to face with the rare behaviour of an animal species, a behavior never seen by anyone but those who know what to look for as soon as they see it. She has quite unexpectedly wandered into mysterious circumstances, one of those unseen moments when that particular animal species rescues itself from extinction.

'They're telling a story,' she says quietly to herself and smiles.

'They're playing,' says her son.

'It's the same thing,' she says and feels something thawing deep within herself. The children's peals of laughter echo all around, bright voices that remind her of the white butterflies that arrive early in the spring.

When she was a child, she made games out of the things that she was afraid of. Then she had nothing more to fear except that the game could come to an end. That she would become so grown-up one day that she wouldn't know how to play anymore.

'C'mon!' she says to her son and whirls him in circles so that he laughs bright, loud laughter. They whirl in ring after ring until they stand in front of the Brandenburg Gate and see where women and men are running out of the Academy of Arts and tagging each other, crazy with joy. In the perfume of spring which has erupted yet once more, only to die again.

They tumble onto one another. Young and old, dignified and uninhibited at the same time. Chock-full of smells and fluids, hunger and thirst, love, pain, pleasure, shame, lust and longing. Each time that someone leans back to argue their opinions, their words turn into white butterflies and flutter away. They jump to their feet and run after the butterflies with invisible butterfly nets. Fall over each other and laugh so loudly that more butterflies fly out of their mouths and fly all around.

She follows, hypnotised by the butterflies. There's a twittering in her when they perch on the bridge of her nose, her shoulders, and the top of her head and rest their wings again. She doesn't dare move lest they fly away, but closes her eyes again and visualises how they cloak her son.

'I'm late for kindergarten,' he says then, loudly and insistently and she comes back to her senses. But too late.

It's already 9:15 when she says goodbye to him with a kiss in front of the kindergarten teacher who watches with a posture of good-natured patience.

He can hardly be bothered to say goodbye, he's so excited to go and play.

So is she.

A Regular

Ignacio B Peña

Harsh light pours out from the shop's glass door, piercing through the night's torrential downpour. A bell rings. Ben enters, escaping the wild spray of the night, the fluorescent light pulling his vision into a sharper focus. The air inside is warm from the ovens behind the counter. He moves heavily up the ramp, the storm still clinging to his clothes, and stops before a uniformed Indian woman at the register.

'Welcome to Dominos, may I take your order?'

Ben leans over the high counter, inclining his head to the Indian woman, as if to disclose a secret. He speaks in a low voice. 'Hi there. So, listen. I've ordered here before. I'm kind of a regular.'

The woman at the counter nods her head. 'Okay.' She waits.

Ben angles his face away, his eyes locked to hers. He drips slowly onto the tiled floor. 'I want to order a pizza. I want to get my usual.'

'Okay sir, what would you like to order?'

'The usual.'

'Sir, I don't know what the usual is.'

Ben quickly shakes his head, having forgotten an important detail. 'Of course, I usually order online. Pepperoni pizza, with extra cheese and extra pepperoni.' The woman at the counter starts inputting his order. 'But listen,' he continues, 'I've got a little problem, and I was wondering if you could help me here.' The woman stops tapping her screen and looks up at Ben.

'It's Thursday. I usually order my pizza on Thursdays after work, as a sort of way to end the week in a comfortable way. D'you understand?' The woman across the counter narrows her eyes a little, her head tilting down. 'It's kind of a comfort, like a tradition. The pizza delivery guy knows me. When I moved, he noticed. He asked me once if I used to live on Farnham. You know? A regular.'

The woman speaks. 'Ok sir, so did you want to order your pizza?'

'I do. So here's the problem. I'm sure you can see that at the moment, I'm a little wet.' Ben stretches his arms wide. The sleeves of his cotton hood shift as they rise, releasing a curtain of raindrops onto the floor. 'I live on Mount Albert, and I missed the last bus to the top.' He lowers his face, in a near whisper.

'So I want to order my usual. But I want it delivered.'

The woman stands still. 'You want it delivery?'

'Yes. Here's the thing. I want to be delivered with the pizza.'

'Excuse me?'

'When you make the pizza and deliver it, I want to go with the pizza from the store to my home.'

'Sir, I don't think we can do that.'

'It's ok, the driver knows me. Remember, I was going to order the pizza anyway. And the pizza is going to where I live. So it makes sense, right? If I'm already here, it makes sense if I go along with the pizza.'

The two stare at each other across the counter, until the Indian woman slowly leans away from the terminal.

'Yes, I suppose that makes sense.'

'Great, so then I'll go with the driver.'

The woman shakes her head. 'No, I mean that makes sense to me, but I'm not sure that we can do this.'

'But I'm a regular. The driver knows me.'

She turns away toward the kitchen, looking for something outside of Ben's sight. 'Let me check with the manager.'

The woman walks away, leaving Ben to drip onto the tile alone. He stands perfectly still, avoiding any unnecessary contact with the cold, hardened cotton draped on his body.

A bell rings.

He turns as the front door opens behind him. A tired young Asian man enters, limply holding an empty pizza bag. The delivery guy. Ben searches the young man's eyes, connects. He smiles and nods, raising his hand in greeting.

'Yo.'

The delivery guy glances back at Ben, his face pulled in confusion. As he walks past he nods his head once, returning no other sign of recognition. He opens the heavy black door leading into the kitchen and disappears.

Ben's hands wilt back into his wet pockets. He leans back against a nearby railing. The Indian woman shuffles back to the register and rests her hands on top of the console, lips pursed.

'Sir, I spoke with the manager. I'm sorry but we cannot allow for this to happen. This is a big company and it would be a safety issue. We cannot be responsible if anything were to happen.'

Ben's stare remains steady on the black door leading to the kitchen. The woman waits a few moments before nervously gripping the register console. The rain outside whips across the windows, a ravenous clawing at the glass.

'Sir, is there anyone that you could call to pick you up?' she asks. Ben continues to lean, his clothes dripping onto his shoes, pooling at his feet. '*Sir*,' she says, more forcefully.

The door's hold on Ben is broken and he turns to look at the woman.

'Sir, did you want to cancel your order?'

Ben stares down at his shoes, darkened by the thirty minutes of wading in the floating river it took to get to where he stood.

'No. Give me the pizza.'

The woman starts tapping the register screen quickly and asks for payment. Ben rummages into his right pocket and unfolds a wet twenty-dollar note, limply scraping it on top of the counter a few times to dry before passing it to the woman. He moves off to the side. The woman disappears into the kitchen, and Ben is left standing in the waiting area alone.

The latch on the heavy kitchen door shifts with a loud snap and opens, disrupting the quiet of the empty shop. The delivery guy strides into the white room and moves toward the exit, a bag full of pizza balancing on his shoulder. He pushes out into the wild night and disappears. Ben stands leaning against a red wall, his stare fixed on the pressing night beyond the glass as he waits. The Indian woman appears from behind the kitchen wall, approaching the counter with a box in hand.

'Sir?'

Ben turns to look at her, the haze of the empty room broken. He takes the hot cardboard box gently, thanking the woman, and walks to the exit, the sound of his wet clothes heralding his departure as he moves.

A bell rings. He exits the shop. She looks on at the door, face pinched into a frown, and absently rubs her arms as if warming herself from a long chill.

The storm continues to pour mercilessly onto the asphalt. Around the corner from the front of the pizza shop, Ben sits in a sheltered bus stop, the glass stained from years of lashing rain. The wind howls steadily through the corridor of buildings before him, the raindrops streaking past like needles. His cheek is sprayed intermittently with a stinging wetness as his right thigh is warmed by the pizza box, his left hand in his pocket, absently fondling his loose change.

Through the white noise of the storm, a rhythmic sound cuts through and pulls Ben's attention to the distant footpath. He turns and sees a large figure ambling to the bus stop, his back bent low. The figure enters and pulls his hood back. A round Samoan face emerges, skin brown and face covered in a deep soot-colored beard. 'Cuz, this weather's *mean*. Hey, you waitin for the bus?'

'Missed it.'

'Aw, stink.' The large man sits next to Ben and stares out at the empty street, his legs swaying open and close underneath his large belly like a bored child. He turns sharply to Ben. 'How far you going, Cuz?'

Ben gestures to the road leading up Mount Albert. 'All the way to the top.'

The large man shakes his head. 'Stink bro, and with this shitty weather. Rough.'

'You?'

The Samoan man opens his arms wide, his heavy coat moving loudly. 'I'm already here!' The large man smiles widely as the wind whips around the small shelter, his heavy mass quivering as he quietly chuckles to himself. The wind howls. Ben looks down at the untouched pizza box on his lap.

'Hey, want a slice?'

The Samoan man looks down at the box in surprise. 'Ohh cuz, for real? I'm hungry *as*.' He reaches for the box and opens it. He looks at Ben, suspicious. 'Bro, you haven't eaten any. This thing safe?'

'Yeah man. I'm just not all that hungry.'

The large man rocks back with a heavy laugh. 'This is my lucky night! Churs, Cuz. Churs.' He takes a healthy bite from his pizza while shaking his head, his eyes smiling at the rain around them. He offers the open box to Ben, but Ben raises his hand, politely refusing. The Samoan man rocks giddily back and forth, finishing his first slice and reaching for another. 'Bro, what a night. Man, what a night!' He drapes his hood over his head and stands, a loud swish of his clothes breaking through the sound of the storm around them. Setting the box on the bench beside Ben, he leaves it half open, reaching for two more slices and stacking them onto the second half-eaten slice in his hand. He slaps Ben on the shoulder as he walks past. The large man exits the bus stop, laughing, trundling into the wild rain as the slices in his hand drown into the darkness with the rest of him.

Headlamps cut through the thick storm and stop just before the bus shelter. The engine stops, cutting the current to the lights. The door opens and from it the pizza delivery guy emerges.

He walks around the hood of the car, his bag empty from his round of deliveries. Just past the bus stop he glances and sees Ben sitting alone with his pizza. He pauses, a look of momentary recognition flashing across his face, before it disappears and he continues into the shop. Ben holds his own gaze onto the ground, his thoughts and his body still.

The uneven scrapes of rain wash across the path in front of the bus stop, measuring the slow stretch of the night. The delivery guy exits and enters the shop three more times. Upon each return he parks his black vehicle a few meters away from the bus stop, not once looking back to the shelter. On the fourth exit, he leaves, and does not return.

The light in the shop goes out, conceding the violent night its victory over the quiet street. Ben sits alone, his damp clothes fused onto his skin like ice, his body numb to the storm's chilled screams blowing through the opening of the shelter. He lowers himself onto the bench, curling into a ball, and places the box just underneath his head. Gently he presses his left cheek onto the lukewarm cardboard square, his eyes shut.

A bell rings. The door opens and the Indian woman rushes past in the rain to her vehicle, cowering in the hood of a large coat. She fumbles in the wind for her keys and drops them on the pavement by the driver side door. As she collects them and looks back up, she sees Ben lying on the bench and stops, pursing her lips as the rain whips into her.

She rustles through the storm away from the vehicle and to the shelter of the bus stop.

'Sir,' she says, too quiet to carry over the howling wind. Ben does not respond. The woman steps closer to Ben and nudges him on the shoulder until his head pops up off the cardboard box, looking around in the dark until he sees the Indian woman standing over him.

'Sir?'

He hangs there, waiting.

'Are you okay?'

Ben lowers his gaze away from the woman to the footpath, letting his head rest back onto the pizza box.

'I'm sorry,' he says.

The woman shakes her head. 'Why?'

She waits for him to respond. He stares into the dark, his eyes darting about as if he were searching for an answer in the rain.

'It was Mount Albert, yes?'

He looks up at her, his attention wrested away from the storm. He nods.

'This rain is terrible. You should be home by now.' She was shivering in her coat. Ben begins to lower his eyes away again but she begins to motion her arms quickly at him, her coat rustling aloud with the hurried movement. 'Sir, it's cold! In my car, hurry up!'

Ben props himself up as the woman turns and shuffles across the footpath and to the driver's side of a dark two-door hatchback. She disappears into the vehicle. Inside, the dome light switches on, casting a deep shadow over her face as she motions again for him to follow. He collects the pizza box from the bench, casts uncertain looks about the street, and crosses the storm, opening the passenger door into the woman's car.

'Sorry, I'm going to get your seat all wet,' he says.

'I know,' she replies.

The two sit in the dark, neither of them speaking, Ben's attention focused on the box on his lap so as to avoid looking at the woman.

'Well?' she asks.

Ben looks up.

'Where are we going?'

'Oh. Um. Buckley. It's on Buckley. Do you know where that is?'

She nods her head in response and sets the key into the ignition, turning the vehicle on and pulling down her seatbelt, clicking it into place. Ben returns his gaze back to the pizza box, saying nothing as she drives the car away from the curb and into the night.

The woman hums a tune as she follows the road. She stops at the first intersection at the top of the ridge.

'It's to the left. Just follow the road past Melrose, it's at the very end of the street.'

She nods, and drives on for a time.

'Right here,' he says, once they reach the end of Buckley Road.

The car comes to a slow crawl and stops. The streetlamps overhead buzz dimly in the night, and from the top of this mountain past the last houses of the road, the world falls away and only the storm remains.

She turns to Ben. 'Sir, will you be okay?'

He nods, a small movement of his head. 'I'm sorry.' He sits still, staring at the dark space under the dashboard where his legs are stretched out. A thought strikes him, and he looks up.

'Say. Do you want a slice? I know it's cold, but, it's not so bad cold, you know? I never really get to eat a pizza with someone else, and. Well. It'd be nice.'

She sits quietly, regarding him for a few moments.

'Okay.' She nods her head. 'Okay.'

Ben opens the pizza box with a measured sense of care, and turns the open box to the woman. She takes a small slice and holds it over her lap. Ben collects one for himself, and closes the box. The two sit with their slices, waiting for each other, until the woman takes a bite from her pizza and starts chewing. Ben does the same, and as he chews he releases a slow breath and his shoulders relax.

'Why are you alone tonight?' she asks.

'I'm alone every night,' he replies through a mouthful of pizza.

'I'm sure that is not true.' He bites into his pizza once more and as he chews she continues. 'It is not true now.' He rests his hands onto the box on his lap and studies her.

'Where are you from?' he asks.

'Mumbai. All my family is in Mumbai. My family. My husband's family. They are all waiting for us there.'

'They're waiting for you?'

'My husband and me, we came to this country because it would be a better opportunity for him, for a little while.' She pauses, searching her words. 'And it has been kind to us. But some day we will go back home. We will not die in this place. It is a beautiful place but it is not our place. I will go back to India one day with my husband and I will die in India.'

She nods her head and takes a bite of her slice of pizza.

Ben looks at her a long while. She turns to him, staring at him in the dark. He looks outside to the rain, his eyes searching the night, gripping the pizza box in his lap.

'I've never heard anyone say that before.'

'Say what?'

'Say where it is they're going to die.'

She looks at him in the steady darkness of the storm. 'Everyone should know where their home is. If they do not know this, then they need to find it. That is my home. That is my heart. That is where I will die.'

She nods once more, and bites into the slice in her hand. Ben continues to look at the woman, sitting calmly in the dark eating pizza in the quieting storm. He turns to look at the raking wind that spills over the city in the dark. He speaks.

'I'm glad you're here.'

The Offset & The Calving

Ryan Vance

Beyond the Ring Road motorway's border of Alaskan lupins, tall and bulbous purple, Edith saw a fat plume of steam puffing from distant rocks to blend into the low clouds, three smaller jets hissing nearby. She imagined the entire world somewhere between a snowglobe and crystal ball. She could shake it, and peer inside, and see herself tossed about, to settle into an unknown future.

'It's so fucking pretty,' she said to June, who was driving them to an ice lagoon. In the steady morning light her round face looked thinner than the version Edith had fallen for, in another time, a different country. Edith shifted her seatbelt into a more comfortable position across her stomach, wondered if an Icelandic lifestyle would have a similar effect on her own stubborn body, too fond of bad habits.

'They're invasive,' said June. 'The lupins. Brought here ages ago, but they're making it difficult for other plants.'

'Okay, Captain buzzkill,' Edith laughed. 'Can we at least get out of town before we crash into reality?'

'I thought it was interesting!' June kept her eyes on the road, but pointed in the general direction of the steam. 'And that over there's a geothermal plant. Or hydroelectric? I'm not sure.'

'You've been here how long?'

'Oh, come on, Edith. Where's your nearest power plant, back home? Do you know?'

Edith didn't appreciate, so soon after her arrival in Reykjavik, the distinction between where each of them called home. Although if you could tell just to look at them both. Edith was wearing her spanking-new hiking boots, old jeans and a bright waterproof jacket, as advised by dozens of tourist websites, while June looked as normal as everyone else around here, wrapped up in simple layers.

'How far away is Juka... Julaca...'

'Jökulsárlón? Three hours, maybe four.'

'Wow, that's longer than it took to fly here.'

'Right,' said June, an edge to the word that suggested Edith was also wrong. The roads were long and straight and challenging in their constancy.

'Thank you, again.'

'It's okay,' said June. 'I haven't been there since I got here. You've got me doing the tourist circuit.'

'Yeah, well, thanks.'

'You don't have to keep saying it.'

Edith knew she'd been unfair on June, showing up unannounced midweek at her work. The shop staff ushered her wordlessly into a basement stuffed with half-finished suits, string, tape and sewing machines. June hadn't been angry to see her, just efficient. Her clipboard of spreadhseets tucked under her arm, she'd scribbled Edith a map to her house. As if she'd forgotten how bad Edith was at spatial things like reading maps. As if she didn't care that Edith had avoided looking at maps since June left.

Because now Edith hated maps. The time difference wasn't too difficult to manage between Iceland and Scotland, but the *distance* distance? All that sea, all those underwater ridges and saltwater clefts? Over months the knowledge of them gathered up into its own impasse, rising from the depths.

After so much silence, and such a practical welcome, Edith was thankful June hadn't asked her to sleep on the sofa. Instead, in June's bed of pale wood and light blue sheets, they'd spooned until they fell asleep, woke up in the same configuration. Just spooning, June's nose to the nape of Edith's neck, June's warm hands holding Edith's soft belly. Nothing else happened. Neither of them wanted it. Everything between them was too fragile, too easily bruised, in the dark.

But here in the car on the road to Jökulsárlón June seemed to have frosted solid overnight. 'So are you going to tell me?' she asked. 'We can stop avoiding it, right?'

'You've been busy, y'know, sorting yourself out here.'

'Eleven months, Edie. I'm pretty well sorted.' No surprise there. Swapping a career in Scottish arts funding for a sales job in Icelandic fashion seemed as simple for her as washing off a facemask. Edith knew the truth wasn't that simple – it took a lot of energy to appear so collected – but couldn't shake the feeling that June led like a frictionless life. As if to prove this true, when she accelerated to overtake three other cars, first one pulled over, then another, then the last.

'Tell me what's going on,' June said. 'You owe me that.'

So as the geothermal plumes faded in the rear-view mirror, Edith vented. The short version was this:

She'd lost her job in the print shop, but they'd been kind enough to pay her the full month's salary, so she'd bought a flight to Iceland. Why not? If her whole life could so easily become shifting sand it made sense to run towards whatever solid ground she could find. And June was solid – wasn't she?

'I assume,' said June, 'The long version maybe elaborates on why they fired you?'

The car crested a ridge, bringing into view a complex of ghost-white, low ceilinged buildings, dwarfed but bright against the rolling expanse of dark rock.

'What're those?'

'You're deflecting.'

'Are they greenhouses?'

'Edith.'

'Okay, yeah, I fucked up.' Edith huffed. Could June really drive for hours across such outlandish scenery and ignore it?

'Isn't printing just pressing buttons?'

'It's like everything else, after a point you have to be precise.'

But that wasn't all. Printers, creasers, guillotines. Such an old invention, you'd think they were simple machines. Not so. Centuries of evolution had heaped complexity upon complexity, transforming simple processes into magic tricks. Calibrations of half a millimetre, applied to one toty sensor hidden deep in clunking, whirring innards, could pull everything back into alignment, make everything right. When the heartless things broke down, men in grease-spattered overalls would hold striped sheets up to the light, pointing out errors so inconsequential, Edith often had to lie and say she could see what the problem was even when she couldn't.

Worst of all had been clearing paper jams, when for no good reason the greedy things would chew up several sheets in one go, clogging their gears and rollers, as if self-sabotaging. The solution was to pinch and tease with tweezers, delicate and patient, until the obstruction cleared.

Edith's preferred solution was to stick her big hands in among the small things, grab and yank and hope for the best. Sometimes things ripped and snapped. Expensive things.

'They didn't like that.'

She looked over at June, who was smiling to herself, eyes still focused on the long road ahead.

'What?'

'Nothing.'

'No, what's funny?'

'Nothing! Hey, let's take a detour,' said June. 'It'll set us back a few hours but you'll get a kick out of it. There should be a map in the glove compartment. Get it out.'

Edith did as directed, too surprised by the change of plan to resent how easy it was to obey June, and be reshaped.

On either side of them the red-brown walls of the North Atlantic ridge stood thirty, maybe forty feet tall. June walked ahead on the boardwalk raised between the cliffs, eager to complete the detour as quickly as possible, but Edith dallied. She felt like a marble lost between old, warped floorboards.

'I can't believe they just let people walk down here,' she said. 'Isn't it still moving?'

Edith looked back at the car, then looked at her watch. 'Seven millimetres every year.'

'Fuck!'

'It's not that much.'

'That's an entire bleed area!'

'A what?'

'Oh, uh, printing chat. The space between artworks on a sheet, it's necessary but we trim it off...' June's face was a bluff, she didn't care. 'Oh, never mind. Doesn't matter.'

Edith had hoped the jargon she'd learnt could be spat out of her head like an ash cloud, but no such luck. Somewhere inside, it had fused to her, and she was now forever going to be surprised at the scale of things. A stack of posters trimmed a whole seven millimetres were destined for the recycle bin. But here, where America and Eurasia rubbed rocky shoulders, two giants sliding against each other hot and sharp? No biggie.

'Sweetie?' June said, foot tapping.

'This was your idea.'

'I know, but it's just rocks. Please. I'd like to be home by midnight.'

Strapped back into the passenger seat, Edith found herself envying the tectonic plates' lack of concern for the delicacy of humans.

*

After an hour of driving, invasive wildflowers gave way to acres of old lava, folded in on itself in solid black bubbles, all coated with a light-green moss.

'This is amazing,' said Edith. It made her feel a little ill. 'It's like... curdled milk on burnt toast.'

'I go this route about once a month, we've a buyer in Fjarðabyggð.'

The road was narrow and rubbled at the edges. With the speedometer reading kilometres rather than miles, Edith had no idea how fast they were really going. But what really baffled her was when the road would occasionally bend. What was the reason? Why not fly straight ahead, what impossible terrain had decided they should turn left, or right, or rise above it all on buzzing cage-metal bridges?

'I don't think I could ever be bored here.'

'You only got in yesterday,' said June. 'You've barely started your holiday.'

'I'm not on holiday.'

The car's tyres scrabbled in the black dirt at the side of the road, and June pulled it back towards the centre line.

'You're not?'

'No.'

'Oh,' said June, and turned on the radio. It provided escape from their crushing silence, until they'd passed through the lava fields. Then the signal became patchy, the presenter's voice fragmenting into shards of language Edith couldn't piece together.

It took effort to break the silence, but there was still wonder in the journey and she would not let it go unremarked upon.

'I mean, *those mountains*! They're shaped like... a sleeping dragon! A head, down to a neck, then back up into a chest and wings. The snout's pointing towards the road. See it?'

'Sort of?' said June. 'There's a nice waterfall on the other side. *Skogafoss.*'

'Jeez, spoilers much?'

The bouldered beast filled their view from their little can of a car. No need to breathe flame if ever it took flight: hot air rushing from under its mile-wide shadow would cloak it in lightning, storms and fury. They rounded the snout. The crashing waters of Skógafoss shone in the afternoon glare, a shimmering tinfoil panel set into earth.

'Nice?' said Edith. 'Nice is nothing! That's magnificent! There's a road! Can we? Can we please?'

'Maybe on the way back.'

'We'll be too tired.'

'I'm not your tour guide.'

'What?'

'I said,' said June, 'I'm not your fucking tour guide.'

Edith's fists clenched of their own accord. 'Pull over.'

'I'm not stopping.'

'I don't mean for the waterfall, June.'

Edith couldn't tell if the rushing sound she heard was the waterfall or the blood in her ears.

'Hold on.' June sighed. 'There's a lay-by just ahead.'

'Just ahead' meant another twenty minutes of driving. The lush mountains crumbled into miles of black sand and grey rubble, eons old ash. The scale of the landscape caused Edith's fury to cool from white hot to a liquid red, crusted over with dark resignation. She was just one angry person, buzzing away in the middle of nowhere.

Edith thought about what it must be like to drive this road twice a month, and wondered if something similar had happened to June, with what had once been between them. Wonderment burnout, feelings fizzling to nothing when presented with so much time and space.

Petty love held out to the stars, unimpressed.

June turned off-road into a gravelled lay-by and parked next to a picnic bench, the only evidence of humanity in sight. Everything felt so futile. They sat inside the car in silence until Edith couldn't take it anymore.

She got out of the car and screamed.

It was windier out here than she had expected, and more full of flies. She waved the bugs away from her mouth and felt silly.

June shut the engine off and stepped out of the car. 'Feel better?'

'No.'

'Sort of stops right in front of your face, doesn't it? Nothing for the sound to bounce off.'

'It's scary.'

They sat down at the table, facing each other, June's expression unreadable.

'What were you expecting?'

'Not an echo. But not that either.'

'No, what were you expecting from me?' June held her hands up to the infinite sky. 'We haven't spoken in weeks. Am I meant to just put my life on hold while you're here?'

Edith shrugged. 'You've done that anyway.'

'I didn't want to! I was getting used to the idea of... you know. Starting over.'

'Ditto.'

Edith looked to the horizon. It seemed as if the grey clouds had been poured between two black mountain ranges, rolling onto the faraway ground like a spill of white paint. 'What's going on over there?'

'What? Oh, that's the glacier. That's where I'm taking you.'

'There!' Edith prodded the table with a heavy finger. 'That's why I'm angry! You're not *taking* me anywhere. We're going together. Aren't we?'

June brushed a fly out of her fringe. 'That's not how it feels on my end. Might be the easiest thing for you, showing up without thinking, but to me this is...'

June chose her next word with care.

'Unsupportable.'

'What does that even mean, June?'

'I have a life set up here. Maybe a few months ago I could have fit you in, but not now.'

Edith stood up and twirled with her arms outstretched. The mountains and glacier and miles of ash spun around her in a grey blur. 'What do you call this? You have plenty room!'

'Stop it.' June snapped. 'Stop being so... We're out here because...'

Edith came to a standstill and let her silence press down on June.

'I don't know what else to do with you! It was a shit idea. I don't... I don't know what else to do with you.'

Oh, thought Edith, is that all? She doesn't know where to go next? But the possibilities were endless! They just had to keep trying, keep butting up against the impossible, until it crumbled or fell over or broke or became clogged up by all their attempts at figuring things out. They could be their own technicians. That was simple. You just had to thrust in your hands and fumble and something would click.

'So we keep going,' she said.

June stared at her, didn't even flinch when one of the billion ash flies landed on her cheek. 'Are you even listening to me? It's over.'

'I meant, we keep going to the lagoon, you dummy.'

Edith tried to smile. A small adjustment.

'Oh, fuck off!' June stood, almost ran to the car. Edith felt the whole world shifting to best suit this effortless woman she couldn't stop crashing into, and only realised she was being ditched at the lay-by when June revved the engine, reversing wheels spitting gravel into the air.

June slid her hands under a large black stone, paused a moment to feel its smooth surface against her palms, then waddled it down to the water's edge. There, she rolled it over so that its broadest, flattest side pointed to the sky, and wiggled its point into the small pebbles underneath. She stood back and hunkered down to check it was level. A mountain, inverted.

On her trips to Fjarðabyggð and back again, she'd stop at the lagoon to build a cairn, adding to the hundreds that lined the shore. Some cairns were so impeccably balanced June suspected their architects had come to Jökulsárlón armed with tubes of superglue. Her own creations never seemed to survive the month between visits.

Looking past the stone she saw the calm surface of Jökulsárlón, under which invisible currents pushed icebergs like toys. The bergs came in all shapes: some smooth and sculpted in meandering white curves, terminating in weird flourishes of gravity; others glowing an ethereal blue; still others flat, gouged and ridged, like gum peeled from a plimsoll.

She'd lied to Edith about how often she came to this quiet place, hoping it would make it feel more new. More like a holiday. A guide boat full of tourists in fluorescent orange lifejackets thrummed between the ice sculptures, disturbing a family of ducks, which grumbled and splashed their way towards June. There were other birds besides ducks at the lake, too, Arctic Terns, small and sharp and white, and others that looked like gulls but weren't, and would throw up on you if you got too close.

Edith would have loved that titbit.

Ditching her at the lay-by had been a good decision, though. The serenity of the lagoon would have been lost on both of them today – lost on Edith almost by default. June imagined her throwing stones at the icebergs, chasing the ducks or singing loud to the sleek seals under the waves, something juvenile like that. Hitch-hiking was also juvenile, so Edith would get back to Reykjavik just fine.

June began to build her cairn. She chose particular stones, wide and flat, stacked them so the cairn could only be toppled in an act of deliberate destruction.

It wasn't that they'd fallen out of love, not at first. The way June saw things, her coming to Iceland was the consequence of an acceleration Edith had yet to recognise, let alone match. A risk, but not as risky as stagnation. Expecting the trend to continue, she'd made a secret pact with herself: if after twelve months of solitude she wanted to backslide into something more comfortable, give a little patience, take some slight disappointment, then that was something she could do.

Trust Edith to appear a month before the pact expired.

Looking up from her cairn June noticed three terns above a nearby iceberg, flapping as hard as they could to stay in place. It was an ugly berg, not too large, about the size of a minibus, shaped like a fist with a thumb sticking out. Strata of black ash marred the thumb's clear ice, frozen recordings of volcanic eruptions from a decade, a century, one thousand years ago.

As June watched, a crack resounded across the water, and the thumb fell with a splash. The terns dove in after it, folding back their wings to pierce the lake and disappear. Two seconds passed before they shot back out into the air, one carrying a small silver fish in its beak. She wondered if the birds had somehow known the berg was about to break apart just by observing it, or listening close.

Then came a new sound, a rushing sort of rumble: the iceberg was turning.

First it rolled towards June, dunking itself face first into the lake. Then it lurched to the left, scooping saltwater up and over itself, before flopping backwards. A tail of electric blue broke the surface, five metres long, compacted and beautiful and pure. Water streamed down its sides, giving it a shimmering, unreal effect, as if it was trying to come into being from nothing.

June stared. Not in all her visits to the lake had she ever seen anything like this.

The iceberg paused in its movements, thinking, feeling itself, understanding what it had revealed. Some rule of buoyancy pulled the blue ridge under again and the fist, now thumbless, punched back to sky. A scatter of ice chips and chunks plopped into the lake.

Now the iceberg contented itself with small turns and reveals, like it was trying on a new dress in front of a mirror.

June looked for someone to share the experience. The shore was bare but for the cairns. Large waves broke upon the shore, and somewhere out there a tern had a bellyful of startled fish. But for how many long years had that ridge stayed submerged? For how many more would she be the only one to know the shape of it?

The dirty chunk of ice that had once looked like a thumb now looked like nothing in particular. Small enough now to obey unseen currents. June followed, tracing its path along the edge of the lake. She knew where it was going. Pulled towards the short stretch of river that led under a bridge, the ice would be jettisoned into the humbling expanse of the North Atlantic Sea. There, salty waves would turn the ice around, deck it on the shore. The beach along this stretch was a photographic negative of somewhere more typically holiday, black sand strewn with white and alien wreckage. This cast-off, soot-stained nub, scarred by cataclysm, smoothed by time, would come to settle there, to melt in the midnight sun.

Feeling herself a mote of dust caught in a beam of light, June wanted nothing more than to see this piece of Iceland returned to itself, and she ran along the shore to keep up, solid, liquid, gone.

Asibikaashi

RA Davis

On Sunday morning, to Jóna's surprise, the dream catcher had caught a dream. She was woken by an unusual sound. She switched on the bedside light immediately and through half-open eyes caught the twitch of feathers and tassles. She threw herself out of bed. In the low light she could hardly see it, could only hear the web thrumming to the thing's struggle. She began to grope in her memory for any image from the last few hours of sleep. She quickly gave up. It was here. Fastened to the catcher like a moth specimin, only alive.

Until that morning, Jóna thought she'd been sold a dud. Not sold, exactly. It was a gift from Helga which Jóna herself had paid for.

One dark afternoon at the end of November, strolling not far from Helga's flat, they had seen dream catchers hanging in the window of that ridiculous shop. It was early days in their relationship. Jóna remembered the moment vividly. She was about to say something about the economic crisis being a factor in the rise of the new-age-bullshit shop. Before she could say it, Helga had said, 'Oh wow! Cool!'

Scanning the window for the least offensive piece of tat, but seeing where Helga's eyes rested, Jóna was forced to conclude: Helga thought dream catchers were cool.

'You ever had one?'

'No,' said Jóna.

Helga grinned. 'I'll get you one.'

'Why?'

'It'll be great. Come on.'

Jóna shrugged. 'What would I do with it?'

'You'll catch dreams.'

In they went, flustering the windchimes over the door, Jóna's nostrils cringing from the sweet tacky fume of scented candles. Watery harps whispered from hidden speakers. They browsed for a while. Only when the old gent behind the counter had put the thing in a bag and hung it on Jóna's outstretched hand, did Helga realise her purse was back at the flat. So it was Jóna's card that went into the machine. She remembered prodding the greasy keys, shielding her PIN out of habit.

'I'll pay you back,' Helga had said. Jóna carried it around all day. That night they stayed at Jóna's place. Helga fished out the dream catcher after dinner, all excited. She stood on Jóna's bed to hook it to the light fitting, then seemed to forget about it as soon as she bounced down onto the bed. Jóna decided to forget about it too, and the money it had cost, as though her day with Helga was some kind of compensation.

Some nights Jóna was instantly, frighteningly aware of the dream catcher. It was like finally noticing, after years of private sedition, a clunky hidden camera in a favourite lampshade. She had to remind herself the thing was not designed to surveille her waking life, only her dreams.

The dream struggled. Watching it strain and exhaust itself against the sticky threads seemed somehow inhumane. Jóna had always considered herself something of a Buddhist. It seemed vaguely compatible with the life of a biologist. She tried not to swat flies or wasps, happier to suffer annoyance than resort to cruelty. In her master's year, in a rotten London flat, she'd coexisted quite happily with a family of mice. Traps, poison, even blocking their ways in, seemed brutal. *Vermin* was a slur. Those things were life. She tried to think of the catching of the dream as a spectacle of the natural world, a privilege to witness; like a heron plucking salmon from a stream, or a hawk hunting on the wind. No victims in nature. In any case, to interfere with the process, to release the dream, would surely damage the catcher. She would hate for Helga to think her ungrateful.

All morning she busied herself with other things: a bath, a long breakfast, reading yesterday's paper cover to cover. She kept the bedroom door shut. When the light came at mid-morning, it only penetrated the front of the flat. The shutters in the bedroom, closed to retain heat, let in no light at all, a mercy in the summer months.

When the necessity of laundry brought her back into the bedroom she intended to ignore the catcher, but could not resist looking. Detecting no movement she thought perhaps the dream had spent itself in the fight. She drew closer, close enough to the see the veins in its translucent wings, lit by the bedside light. It buzzed angrily and made her jump. She left the room like she was leaving an argument. How long would she have to wait?

It buzzed for the next hour, on and off. She went out to the shops. When she returned it was still going. Gradually, as afternoon quickly became evening, its efforts became less sustained. Later, as the thought of sleep approached, the sound was coming once every few minutes, like a smoke alarm warning of a low battery. If she wanted to sleep, she would have to move it out of the bedroom – a process she was not willing to contemplate – or sleep in another room.

Creeping into the bedroom, she dragged the duvet and pillows from the bed and carried them in a bundle to the living room. She readied herself for sleep, closed the door and lay down on the sofa.

zz.

It was hardly a sound now, only a fractional disturbance of the air, like hearing the radio in the house next door. Was she even hearing it, or was her brain placing the idea of sound where she expected it to occur? She had work in the morning. Imagining that she might not be able to sleep stimulated something; fight or flight. Now she was sure she would not sleep. She reached out in the dark for the light switch, then her phone. She called.

'Hi. I know it's late. Do you mind if I come over?'

On Monday night she offered to make dinner at Helga's place, a thank-you for the sudden sleepover the night before. She stopped by her own place only to check on the dream. Still there. She watched it for a while and observed no sign of life, yet she knew the thing was alive. In the air was a faint ringing of electricity, like an old TV on standby.

She took wine to Helga's, drank two glasses while she cooked and another in front of the TV. Helga said 'Stay' so she stayed.

Tuesday was their usual night together and she went straight from the office. It was late when they ran out of shows to watch. Jóna had everything she needed for work the next day, so once again she stayed. On Wednesday they argued.

They'd met after work, at Jóna's suggestion. Helga was irritable from the moment she sat down, complaining about the Christmas music playing in the bar. Jóna took her up on the argument if only to let it run its course and be done. Jóna finally apologised, somehow able to take responsibility for the offence, while at the same time blaming it on the alcohol. Finally they parted for the night, at the same street corner where they had said goodnight after their first ever date.

'Goodnight Jóna.' Helga kissed her quickly and turned away in a puff of breath.

Jóna listened as the crunch of Helga's footsteps on the thin layer of new snow faded away.

Arriving back at her house she was annoyed to find that the small holly wreath she had hung on the front door, her only concession to the Christmas season, had fallen from its hook. She shook off the snow and replaced the wreath, then let herself in. She tore off scarf, gloves, coat and scrambled out of her boots. When she was well inside and getting warm she sat at the kitchen table and opened her laptop. Within minutes she had formed a basic understanding of the dream catcher.

It was a filtration system, she concluded: good dreams passed through the web, bad dreams were snared. Her dream was a bad dream. She read more. The dream catcher originated with a tribe whose people had become dispersed across North America. With the people spread out, the spider woman who brought the sun each day was working harder and harder to reach every corner of the continent. The arrival of the sun was known to expel bad dreams. So the women of the tribe wove webs to filter the dreams of their children, to aid the sun in banishing the bad ones. The dream catchers did not dispose of the the dream, they only made the spider woman's job a little easier.

All at once Jóna thought of the tectonic plates of the earth. She thought of the Mid-Atlantic Ridge running through Iceland like an ancient scar; through Þingvellir, where they were taken as school children and shown the rift between continents, the North American Plate parting year by year from the Eurasian. As a kid raised on American movies, it thrilled Jóna to imagine half of Iceland sitting on the sharpened edge of America – it was almost as thrilling as knowing Leif Erikson had got to America before Columbus.

Here they were, on the border between two of earth's facets. And at the same time, they were on the edge of darkness, barely visited by the sun in this, the grip of winter. Even if she opened the blinds tomorrow and let in the weak winter light, what would happen? What could the dream withstand? Jóna knew little of entomology, arachnology, or whatever this was. She knew about fish, ecosystems and fisheries, so her thoughts turned to nets. She froze. What if the dream catcher was as indiscriminate as a fishing net? What if this creature was not its intended prey? What if it was bycatch?

She stood up suddenly. Only then did she realise that since getting home she had not heard the slightest buzz from the bedroom. She took three quick strides to the bedroom door and pushed it open, flicking on the light switch at the same moment. The room was exactly as she had left it. The dream catcher hung motionless. The dream lay spread-eagled across its web.

The dream was clearly dead. Whatever mystery had once posed the wings and tiny legs was simply absent. Its natural mechanism had unwound, leaving it slack and twig-like. Jóna was disgusted. She wished to be rid of it immediately, to conquer her irrational distaste, lift it off the dream catcher, take it to the kitchen and drop it in the rubbish bin; or better, march to the bathroom and flush it down the toilet. She hesitated. Why not get rid of the whole thing: prey, catcher and all? She climbed up on the bed, reached up to the lampshade. Unhooking the dream catcher, she tilted the main hoop to keep the dream from falling, though it was stuck fast. She held the hoop carefully, felt absurdly pompous, like she was holding the Wimbledon Ladies Singles trophy, and stepped down onto her bedroom floor. Marching into the kitchen she flipped up the lid of the big Ikea bin. A mixture of peelings and coffee grounds at the bottom of the bin gave off a sharp vegetable smell.

A knocking came from the front door.

She knew it was Helga from the percussion of her knock. She closed the rubbish bin and went through the inner door to the porch, still holding the catcher. Opening the front door, a blast of cold air rushed at her from the street. Helga did not wait to be invited in, stamping snow from her boots she stepped over the threshold and closed the door behind her. She was out of breath.

'I'm sorry,' she said, unwinding her scarf. 'I just –'

Helga saw the dream catcher, unconcealed at Jóna's side.

'What are doing with that?'

'It caught something. It's OK, it's dead. But now I don't know what to do with it.'

Helga had taken off one glove to knock on the door. She held out her bare hand. Jóna passed her the catcher. They both looked at the dead catch.

Jóna didn't like the silence. 'Do you know what kind of dream this is?'

Helga shook her head.

'I think there's a spider woman from America coming with the sun,' Jóna said.

'Oh.'

Helga tipped the catcher this way and that, like it was a precious antique. Then she turned around and opened the door. She lifted the Christmas wreath from its hook and hung the catcher in its place. She closed the door and handed Jóna the wreath.

'It's for the best,' said Helga.

They went inside.

The wind passing down the street lifted the catcher now and then but did not dislodge the dead dream. The snow fell in the night, even resting on the threads of the catcher and the thin carcass of its prey.

When Jóna and Helga left the flat under the streetlight early the next morning, neither looked back. At about eleven o'clock, the grey glow in the east grew to true morning and lit the quiet street and in that vague winter dawn, eight legs made a loom.

Beyond This River Life May Flow Again

SR Mackison

In the pitch black of night I can hardly see anything. This is the coldest I have ever been. My entire body is shaking from cold; I can hear my bones rattle inside my body. I'm wearing my jeans and my new trainers with the long white jacket that my sister gave me for my birthday. I have my thick and wooly hat on and my scarf wrapped around my face. The bone-piercing cold of this night makes me feel like I'm naked.

I take my right hand out of my pocket and touch my face; I don't feel anything. My senses are freezing. I put my hand back into my pocket. At this moment I'm not thinking about anything. My mind feels so empty.

I can hear them breathing, but I can't see their faces. I'm sitting on the ground, it must be muddy; I can feel the moisture penetrating through my jeans and jacket reaching my flesh.

In the far distance I see the trafficker coming with a torch in his hand. As he is walking towards me he casts the light on the rows of refugees sitting right next to me. For a second or so I can see their faces. Tens of men and women dressed in black sitting on a muddy pasture with their faces covered with their scarves. Some of them have blankets with them; I can also see their bags and suitcases lying on the ground. The beam of his torch glows brighter as he approaches me. He flashes the torch into my face. I can see his face now, for the first time. It's hard to distinguish his dark features from the dark of night. He has a long face with a large pointy nose and bushy dark eyebrows. The wrinkles along his cheeks and forehead are so deep that they look like scars.

He looks at me and with a broken voice says:

'Hey you, your coat is not black, take it off. Right now. They will find us. Then he looks at Mahlon and shouts 'Tell your sister to take it off.'

His voice is so deep and husky that gives me a sense of unknown fear that I've never experienced before. I look at Mahlon who is sitting next to me.

'Mahlon, what is he saying? Take my jacket off? Is he insane? I'll die.'

Mahlon looks into my eyes; in a fraction of a second we can both sense what the other is thinking about. Mahlon's face is so pale, his lips look so dry and cracked in the corners, and his nose is runny. I look into his eyes again; I feel a sharp pain in my chest.

'Take it off and put it in your backpack', he says. 'Hurry up. Hurry up. You can wear my coat instead.'

As I'm hurriedly unbuttoning my jacket with my numb fingers I say,

'I don't need your jacket, what do you have under your jacket? Just a stupid t-shirt? This cold will kill you.'

The trafficker hits me on the face with his torch murmuring 'hurry up, hurry up' and walks away.

Mahlon comes closer to me and touches my face.

'Naomi, this guy is crazy. Our life is in his hands we have to listen to him.'

'I'm okay; I'm not cold anymore. I don't feel anything.'

Then we sit back where we were. I hug my backpack between my legs; I pull it against my body to give me some heat. This cold is unbearably painful. As I lean over my backpack I can feel the cold climbing my spine like a ladder, it goes up right to my neck and then enters my skull and dulls my thoughts.

'My heart is freezing Mahlon.'

'What?'

'My heart, I said, it's freezing.'

'Can I do anything about it?

'No, Nothing.'

Then we both become quiet and listen to the trafficker who sits on his knees and addresses everybody:

'From now on I want everybody to keep their mouths shut. Not a single word I want to hear. Not a single word. Understood? We are just behind the border security post, less than half a mile away there is a boat waiting for you. As you pass across the river you will be in a new country. Just behind this stone wall in front of you is the security building. If they catch you, they will send you back. Did you get what I said? You just follow my voice and me.'

I look at Mahlon. He holds my hand and murmurs 'we will be fine'. I don't know what I should feel like right now. I don't know if I'm scared or I'm confused.

He starts walking towards the wall and we follow him. A few steps alongside the wall there is a big hole in the wall. We bend and pass through the wall. There he stops everybody and quietly says:

'Run after me. When the spotlight scans near us and I know the time is right I'll shout 'Lie down', I want you to lie down, immediately! If they see one of you, they will catch all of us and will send us to jail, and I swear I'll kill that one person with my own hands.'

In a far distance I can see the spotlight search the landscape. I can see the scenery; it's a patchy green field with ups and downs.

He gives us a couple of seconds to get ready. I hold Mahlon's hand and look at the starry sky. Mahlon draws closer to my ear and quietly says:

'This is the end of the journey. Beyond this river there are no fears. Beyond this river we can find a new home. Beyond this river life may flow again.If we just made it to the other side of this river, we would breathe freedom into our suffocated lungs. If we only made it to the other side of this river'

'Do you think we can make it Mahlon?'

We stare at one another, then look at the cross-like stars shining above our heads. Then I hear the trafficker calling, 'ok everybody get set and run after me, don't forget that if they catch you that will be the end', then I look at Mahlon and for the last time I ask him, 'do you think we can make it?'

Peripheries

Arun Sood

It can be disorientating
to be on the peripheries
of two plates of heritage.

High in McLeod Gang
I slurped Thali in ignorance
of Sir Donald Friell, knighted:

'The Most Exalted Order of the Star of India'.
A Highlander in Himalayan hills,
one hundred years earlier than I.

I remained, though, a pale virgin
seduced by Shiva's curving mounds,
blessed by echoes of Buddhist bells
but, nevertheless, alone in the smoky valleys.

Some years later, I stirred again
Kedgeree – simmering in Ardnamurchan,
the white flakes of Hebridean Mackerel,
sparkling midst wild brown basmati grains.

Unsure, still, of which might be mine
I straddle the peripheries; with no plate
or knife, or fork, or finger
to wean the hunger of belonging.

Inertia

Valgerður Þóroddsdóttir

Not lack of movement, but a steadying
between bodies.

I wake to find the things I couldn't say in the dream.

The space between train and platform
like the space between this night and the last

where you wait with ink-stained fingers,
water-stained mouth.

Between us, an interval
that separates now from the canal.

It's not the distance
between here and there
that is unbridgeable.

We live this moment across years.

The pull between planets
that approach but never meet.

in

Vala Þórodds

touching
the periphery
excited, finally
about something beyond the real

(what happens with the body
always being like a secret
we carry within)

the light of morning draws lines
hinting at the shapes of things outside

(as in the dream
where your mother
is not your mother

the face not hers
but breasts
insinuating
and tongue)

anticipation grows
out of everything

desire burrows outward
from shadow
brutal, clean as a mirror

Tattoo

(after Edwin Morgan)

Ian Burgham

Elephants in a circle
trunk to tail travel
her skin. Somehow within the herd
they sense something about to be born.

How hard it had become to live.
Then, to have found her
in a room, the smallest of space
became an everywhere.

The furniture is carpets, tables,
lamps and chairs
but the wide expanse of thought
is measureless –

her hands, fingers, nails –
strange birds sing
amongst flowers and thorns
in the wallpaper ivy.

Abstractions appear
till the sun is ripped
from distance, the world –

plunged into darkness,
the light of tamed flame
brought down, crushed, mixed
by mortar and pestle

to pour new light into word
sculpted in a poem's canvas
becoming my shameless lover,
her nude body, its fuse-force,
its elephant tattoo.

For this refusing to abandon love
and all its strange explosions,
I've abandoned gravity –
Elephants, and within the herd,
the sense of something about to be born.

Spring Vessel
from Three Sestudes
Carol McKay

—A response to work by Canadian ceramicist Andrea Piller

For three days in a lifeboat on that hostile grey ocean
my grandfather ached for earth without water:

footprints pressed in the white sands at Barra;
Ontario flatlands beyond the St Lawrence.

Cupped in waves, his clay heart brimming,
he dreamed of migrants, merchants, home-coming.

Flux, glost and glimmer: a full moon glazing
the cold hulls of vessels all North Atlantic drifting.

Màiri

Andrew McCallum

for Arnaldur Indridason

She was a wee bairn,
settin alane on the shore o a loch,
herknin ti the whisper frae the watter.

Syne she was a quine, leukin oot on the loch
an seein its bonnieness
an the licht that seep't frae oot it.

Syne she was an auld wummin,
hunkert aside a bairn;

syne she was the wee bairn aince mair,
herknin ti the whisper,
an ettlin the forgie o the wuirds;
an the whisper cairrit frae the watter
an the whisper said - *My bairn*!

The Ascension o Minnie Paton

Andrew McCallum

for Morten Veland

The snaa on the hoose is blae in the munelicht.

The trees are bleck an naikit.

Ane auld wummin staps graithly alang the ruif,
ane fuit shooglin aither side o the rig,
til her tremmlin haun gruips the lum
an the weir o her tauchtness sleckens.

Her sark cams aff owre skin an bane.
There's a dunt in her chist.
Her spirlie airms growp ahint her back,
as her spinnle fing'rs hunt the howe atween her shoothers.
She powks at the humf whaur her wings are lirkit.

The wings are nae metaphor.
They're strynge wabbit flesh indrawn agin the cauld.
She onfaulds them caunnie.
Her back loups as they rax, girnin,
the wey her knees jarg i the mornin,
an she spreids them oot ti dry i the lum-reik.
A million capillaries scart a wab o flicht.
Her hert swalls an daurk bluid fluids ti stech them.

The wings pou lik a kite.
They snouk the air lik tethert dugs.
She rowes a scaurf aboot her hausebane,
then haps a rauchan roun her breist.

Whan she hales hersel intil the skyrie nicht,
it's nae less a wunner.
For she daesnae flee eith.
Insteid, she sprauchles hersel upwart,
kickin an scraiblin lik a puddock.

Arctic Roll

Kerrie McKinnel

The knife presses through your beige skin, and slips
down into your core.
You wait, predictably silent, for someone to approach you.
You are the same as a thousand others
in kitchens across Scotland,
dressed up with fruit
to look like a respectable pudding, or laid bare,
cut open for all to see.
Your heart, still frozen,
pushes back against the knife.
Your cardboard shell told me that two hours in the open
air would be enough to soften you,
but your clothing has lied. It will take a full evening in my company
before you give in.

O Cristo Redentor

Andrew McCallum

Nou thon's a muckle Jesus.

It's no hou I ken hím at aa.

Fancy leivin ablo a faither lik thon!

Leuks lik he's barrin the door.

I dae this fur you, ma son.

Leuk, man!

The real Jesus niver groud that auld.

An he wis skinny.

I haudit hím aince in The Seik Kids.

I cud feel hís ribs.

Hís hert hammert lik a spreckle-thrappelt throstle.

I've felt the win frae hís wíngs sin syne.

This muckle theme-pairk messiah

– this isnae Jesus.

The real Jesus pleys a fiddle,

couerin híssel roon the music lik a gourd,

hís skin broun an smellin o cínnamon.

Rio, July 2014

Journey

Rob A Mackenzie

This the 21.51 train from Hyndland to Edinburgh.

The hospital has a B6 ward on the third floor.

The station before Drumgelloch overlooks an Aldi.

When I eat a McDonald's burger, I eat death, I summon death.

This is not my truth or your truth but certainty.

I will reach Waverley station at 23.21.

A station whose name I can't recall overlooks an ASDA.

When I eat a Marks & Spencer falafel and spinach wrap, death is near.

If I believe the train will crash, arrival is a bonus.

The only reason to rejoice is if an outcome was uncertain.

The body in the hospital, small and cold and quiet, was my father.

This is certain, this is truth, but the last thing it feels like is certainty.

Dark Horse

Russell Jones

On summer nights this city's rarely dark.
The sun's an insomniac child, glancing out
from the curtain of clouds. Soon, it will swim
over hidden corners, tease blossoms from buds,
show us our boundaries, shorelines and caves.

I live for darker days, drape a scarf over my shoulders,
walk into the empty, early morning, fold into shadows.
My fists and feet harden into hoofs, I brush my hair
into a mane, spine cracking into a saddleless back
as my tail grows long, sweeps litter from the paths.

I test the miles a horseman can run,
the cobbles fissuring beneath my track,
launch my new legs through the neighbourhoods.
The city is woken to my clops – each inhabitant
wears whatever's closest on the hook, swings
their door, takes to the street, a horseman's word
trotting on their lips. Shetland grey, Coffin Bay white,
Hokkaido and Exmoor; they transform, and the city
is overrun with horses, quick and untamed.

Before the alarms sound, we return home,
steed heads receding on our pillows, mare legs
shortening, hoof to foot, snorts softening to snores.
Everyone wakes with the wind in their blood,
dresses for the day, our suits and minds unstabled.

By insisting on love we spoil it

(Jack Gilbert)

Russell Jones

To sit is enough, so we do: on the too-big sofa,
a coast train, in hookah cafes, minds like smoke
and buttered fingertips. Ask for a shadow and I'll cast it
for you. In the house we bought together, our nursery
is unlikely to be filled. Fine, soon we'll see the green light
of Borealis through the toilet window. Let's tear the sky
down but be assured – unknowing isn't the half of it.
The universe is tiny if we call it out; but each fold
makes another crease we've not yet explored.

Shapinsay

Stewart Sanderson

under the name
a sheepish sigh
a ship at sea
a shapeless sowing

The Resurrection: Port Glasgow[1]

William Bonar

Steer yersel, Faither!
Fling aff the croodit clay
juist hou Stanley Spencer
pictured it, lang syne,
daunderin uit the Glesca Road
betimes in the gloamin,
when his daft vision wis oan him,
the nichts the bombers didnae rin.

Mon wi me up the brae.
Ma Mither's lyin up yonder
douce n qhate nou her stour's
played uit. We'll lea her in the clay.
It's your lugs Ah'd deave!
Ah've a wheen snash tae boak
that micht dae ye guid tae hear.
Forby, ye've naethin else nou tae dae.

Ach, whit keech's this ah'm comin uit wi?
This is fur ma ain sel!
Bi whit richt cin Ah, ten year
yer senior nou, haun ye snashterie?
Ye dune yer best n yer waur
wi whit ye kent, n there wis luve
in it, though we cin baith ain it nou,
in yer hairt, ye didnae care fur me.

N ye couldnae help showin it.
Ye'd cry me *limmer, get, tin man,*
gull, gowk, gawk, boak, n *scunner;*
know-all n *know-naethin; tit,*
erse, diddy n *glaiket* n fell near
throattilt me mair than wance,
hid ma Mither no pult ye aff me.
Nae wunner her hairt wis roastit.

Ye wur ay teuch as girssled butcher meat
tae ma face. Bit wan nicht
yer mask dissolved in whisky.
As Ah lay courin in ablow the sheet
Ah heard yer glaikit splore:
Ma boay won the cup!
Bit neist mornin neither cheep
nor blink, joukie in yer seat.

Ye ken whit? Ah unnerstaun.
Ye hud a script in yer heid
that ye tuik fur hou things are.
Nae duit Ah wis thrawn
n kent better than abody.
We get wan shoat at this an awa.
Maist o it's warslin wi waant
n we dae it aw alane.

Sae it's uirs tae mak a kirk
or a mill o it n Ah've grund it uit.
Ye'd hae nae flechts o fancy
n Ah've brocht ye nane. Through the mirk,
gin ye cud keek, the shipyairds
aw bit gane, the Mill Dam
drained, the Unions stroant oan.
They've erased yer mark.

Sae wi me, Faither. Ah'll gang
the same raid. The licht flichters.
A man's no a man nae mair
bit a libbit stirk cairryin the can.
Awa n streke uit in yer cauld bed.
There's naethin you nor Ah cin dae.
The hail clanjamfrie's singin
the vera last verse o it's sang.

¹ Stanley Spencer's similarly titled painting came from a vision while walking by the steep braeside cemetery in Port Glasgow.
He used faces of people he had known in Port Glasgow, where he was assigned to record war work in the shipyards, as models
for the people scrambling whole from their graves. For Spencer, the resurrection was a universal event that inevitably had
to consist of local manifestations.

These walking blues

Ellen McAteer

On the Partick side
of the Clyde tunnel
a lantern of lives
flickers TV blue
eyelid red

*She's dead
quiet when
she's no oot
bevvyin*

Freedom is bad
for the liver
the moon an acid grin

The river comes
in dark and drunken
waves. Save us. Sing
*I'm wild about that
thing.* Head full of sound

it's no wonder
you were nearly
drowned. Seagulls
with dinosaur eyes
reel above, nesting
between warm lives

the figure of eight
being walked all night
is followed by an inky gaze
a hooded crow scrawks
WhereareyeFAE?

Mine was the most healthy negative space one could discover: so much so it was the opposite of negativity where negativity is an unpositive element. Anne was the direct opposite, and inside my head she was like that. My head had been full of vile bitterness, a composition of bitterness and anger.

Words and Things to Sip
James Kelman

Words and Things to Sip

James Kelman

I had to move on. The main question concerned Anne: where was she? I gave up the highstool at the bar and carried my drinks and bag to a table, accompanied by my brains. That was alright; I needed them to think and I was wanting to think.

The nature of the thought, the content. Forget one's father. Had I been thinking of my father? Not in so many images, simply a sensation, a sensation of daddy – poor old fucker, dead for the last twenty years. We think of the dead, even fathers, they are always with us. Even when we are thinking about all these hundred and one different and varied matters, business matters: will one ever make a sale again in one's entire miserable existence? Shall I ever walk into some fellow's office and chat him into an irreversible decision in regard to a sum of money large enough to guarantee one's job for another fucking month. No wonder one sighs. My old man never had such crap to put up with. He was a factory worker. One contends with all sorts, all sorts.

Life is so damn hectic, especially the inner life. The dead and the undead. And thoughts of Anne and myself, our relationship.

I groaned again. These days I groan out loud. People hear it and look at me.

I didnt need pubs like this in which to become annoyed. Although they did annoy me. I get annoyed at myself, by myself and for myself. Leastways irritated, I become irritated, breathe in breathe out.

Having said that, I was turning over a new leaf. The short-tempered irascible chap had gone forever. Recently I had been prescribed aspirin; anti-coagulants. One's blood. Henceforth I was to be a changed man, a veritable saint of a fellow. Never more would I lose my temper over something as trivial as bad service in a hostelry of questionable merit, a bad boozer in other words, who cares? Not me. Never more. Those parties who ignore a body they perceive as a stranger. Erroneously as it so happens. Little did they know I was a fucking regular so why not treat one as a fucking regular? Who cares, of course, me or not me, it dont matter.

Unpunctuality whether in barstaff or one's nearest and/or dearest.

A bad choice of language. But never more, never more.

What never more? What the hell was my brains on about now? These whatyacallthems did not deserve the name. Brains are brains. Whatever I had, tucked inside my skull, those were unclassifiable, certainly not fit to be described as 'brains'.

Oh god, God even.

Yet Anne was rarely punctual. Why worry about one's nearest and/or dearest.

Odd. I recognised where I was sitting. This was where I typically sat in this typical bar, of all most typical bars. It was side on to the door, avoiding unnecessary draughts.

I had books and reports, the smartphone alive to the touch, even sensing the touch. And an old newspaper too, a – what the hell was it, a something Planet – what a name for a newspaper! Was that not Superman, here at the Daily Planet with Clark Kent and that old chap, the irascible editor, what the fuck was his name? Who knows, who cares, Perry Mason or some damn thing, so what, I could have read the sports pages.

Maybe I would. Whether I did depended. I was drained – drained! Yes, washed out, exhausted, weary, deadbeat, shattered; stick adverbs in front or behind, all you like any you like; mentally, psychologically, physically, sexually, emotionally, socially; then quantify: totally, wholly, almost, just-about, a small amount, very much. Had I strength to spare I might read a report, book or newspaper. Alternatively I could sit and sip alcohol, insert the earplugs and listen to something, something! Or view television, or watch the world go by, neither intrigued nor bored by thoughts of a downbeat nature. Mum too – if it was not the old man it was her – why was I thinking so much about my parents? Maybe I was about to drop dead and that was a sort of roll-call of one's existence. Hells bells.

Anne would be here soon anyway. It did not matter if she were late. I had not seen her for six weeks, had not slept with her for my gad three months, three months. One could ruminate upon that. I enjoyed lying with her side on, her eyelids flickering. She also with me. Twas our favoured position. We relaxed. I did anyway, being without responsibility for eight or nine hours, barring texts, emails and even phonecalls for heaven sake, but I could not switch off the phone, though her breasts, her breasts.

I disliked myself intensely. Nevertheless, one continues to exist. A small something in my pocket. A piece of jewelery nonsense for the one I loved. Gold, gold I tell you gold! I screamed it hoarsely, in the character of a crazed Humphrey Bogart, unshaven, unkempt – what was the movie? the mountains and gold.

Anne liked gold. Women do like gold. Golden jewelery. Joo ell ry. I kept the piece in my trouser pocket that none might steal the damn thing. England was not Scotland. Given that forgetfulness was a greater risk than theft. If I took it out my pocket I would forget to return it.

But I did enjoy gazing upon gold. Gold was a pleasure of mine too given that in my position I could not aspire to the unkempt unshaven look, being as how the state of one's dress, the label on one's suit, the subtlety of one's timepiece

Oh my dear lord. Panic panic panic.

Defective memory banks. The mind dispenses with petty data. The clock on the wall. I checked my wristwatch against it, and the phone checking both, pedantic bastard. And not panicking. Never panicking. Never, never never never. I was not a panicky fellow – never used to be – besides which the anti-coagulants, lest the dropping dead factor... Jesus christ I groaned again! I was glaring, why was I glaring? I studied the floor. One's shoes. One's socks. Tomorrow was Monday and I would buy new ones, new socks.

Oh god god god.

Three gods = one God, the way, the truth etcetera etcetera, breathing rapidly several intakes of what passes for air, for oxygen because one's head, one's brains, what passes for the thingwis, the whatyacallthems.

Where however was she? One would have expected punctuality.

And the barstaff:

barstaff are typically interesting. We try not to study them too blatantly lest personal misunderstandings arise. But we do study people. We are people and people study people. Humankind is a reflective species. Two had been serving in this pub for as long as I had been using it which for heaven sake was a long time; seven or eight years. Certainly a long time for barstaff to remain in the job. They assumed they had never seen me before. They were wrong.

But who wants to be a regular? It means one is alcoholic, near as damn it, an alcoholic geek, one who gets sozzled in the same bar year after year.

Neither bar worker allowed me a second glance. I was a nobody. They might have qualified this to "nobody in particular" which would have been better in the sense that a particular nobody is better than a general nobody. Still it would have been wrong.

Regularity need not operate within a brief span of time; twice every two years is also a pattern, and such an event can be enclosed by mental brackets. I might only have come to this pub six times a year but I only came to the damn town on said half dozen occasions. So is that not regular? Make the question-mark an exclamation. Six out of Six is not 99% but a fucking hundred if one may so speak. Of course I was a regular. Some people are so constipated their bowels only move once a month. But at least it is not irregular.

That crack once landed me an order. They were feeling sorry for me. Once a month every month is measurable, is regularity. A hundred percent. A man had his dick cut open without an anaesthetic. Having to have one's dick cut open! Oh God. One could only shudder. Without an anaesthetic! That was just like – wow! Why even had it come into my mind! But it is such a fact; its incredible nature has it jump into one's mind appropros of nothing whatsoever. It was in the papers, stuck away on page 7, 8 or 9. It should have been front page news. I must have been reading a quality. Unless it was a lie. Even a sexual disease, a serious one: none requires that sort of operation, a severing of the skin. Getting one's penis sliced open without an aesthetic. Dear lord.

Move on move on.

Sliced was my word, not the newspaper's. It just said cut, cut is cut, sliced is sliced and severing is, of course, servering, he intoned gravely.

One considers punctuality. Why?

The main question: why did Anne even consider a fool like me? It was beautiful she did but why? I was no looker, I was no nothing.

Truly, I was not. Yet she had considered me.

Come the cold light of morning this question continued to arise, to haunt my very being as the author of Gothic yarns would have it.

I had one daughter. We never communicated. She used to tell me the books she was reading but due to my cricial commentaries she stopped doing this, and stopped telling me about movies she enjoyed, plays she appreciated, painters that

forget it. The main question, or should I say answer, to our lack of communication forget it.

The only reliable method of knowledge is literature. I was a reader of books. Truth comes in books: we cannot trust internetual information, nor other human beings, obviously, given the chap sitting at the next table to me was reading a quality newspaper so-called, given that in hostelries of this nature such newspapers, not to beat about the bush.

But what could Anne ever see in me? In the final analysis I was a prick. Upon my tombstone let it be writ: Here Lieth a Prick.

Prick rather than dick; dick is a pleasant term.

In contemporary jargon I would admit to having 'fucked up' my life. One should admit such matters and not conceal them if such issues are thought to be the ones, the main perhaps questions, while Anne herself, she was never a blinding flash, what do they call it, love at first sight, oh this is the girl for me, it was not like that. I was in sore need of female companionship. Males tire me eventually. On guard and have at thou. An acquaintance of mine was fairly camp, well, really a friend rather than acquaintance and not 'fairly camp' but wholly so if not blatantly. Male company exhausted him. He told me that. I was pleased he trusted me enough to so confide. I didnt wonder: how come this guy is telling me such stuff? Rather I confessed to a parallel feeling. He nodded, not at all surprised. I appreciated that somebody else felt the same even although I caught him observing me during a lull in the conversation. I respected our friendship but distrusted it. Certainly there were times male company repelled me. Males are uncharitable. Younger males too, perhaps especially. One would expect tolerance. Walking into some factory or warehouse and them all looking and sniggering, what is he selling, fucking fool.

On occasion I need to sit, only to sit, to sit still, to sit at rest, to just be be be be, just be, and unaware of my breath. Without a woman this was impossible. Another friend was an ex-alcoholic and divorced. He told me the major boon concerning alcoholic friends is how they relax together; they share basic acquaintance, occasionally drink tea together, occasionally not. But they lapse into silence. They do. I found that remarkable. I should have expected a headlong charge into confession, each outshouting the other, listen to me listen to me, the poem of course, who was that now? Coleridge.

Silence. The leaves doth grow, doth shed, falling.

I first met Anne on the other side of town. She was in company. I was introduced to her and we got on. We met the following evening. The sexual attraction was mutual. My heart skipped a beat. What is beat? The assignations began and we lay together. She chose the rendevous. This bar.

Life has the habit of booting one in the testes. Anything might happen. I checked my watch and, instinctively, my belongings. A man had risen from his seat, cigarette already in his mouth, making for the smoke exit. He was a shifty looking buggar. An older man but older men can be shifty given they are less suspicious, immediately that is. Once one ponders a little one has second thoughts, these bastards are just cautious, seeking the slightest opportunity.

The truth is that I did not care. If someone wished to steal my goods and chattels they were most welcome because I did not give a fucking shit one way or the other and that is to be blunt about it.

I had become an afternoon drinker, an imbiber of false hopes, false dreams. Even one's fantasies are false. What is a false fantasy? I once had a boozy conversation with my daughter. Unfortunately I advised her of my secret desire which, at that time, was death. Nothing false about that.

Oh fuck.

I reached for my briefcase to check the report. I had 'a report'. A REPORT!

Jesus god.

I also had an anthology of short stories by writers from Central America. I left it concealed. Instead I would read the walls and read the tables, read the chairs and read the floor. Truths are where you find them.

I opened the report once again, he sighed wearily.

The sort of fucking garbage one is fed at head office. Not that I cared, I did not fucking give a fucking rat's fucking arse, bastards. Even if they did fire me. I did not fucking care. Not one solitary particle for all their lies and dissembling: should one be cast onto the heap of forgotten souls? Never!

They no longer pretended respect. But I had none for them so there we are. Whatever I had was gone. Such incompetence. They were unable to back a chap! They wanted to sack me but could not. Ever heard anything like that! At my age, all one seeks is competence, efficiency. People who do their work in a consistent manner. They do not fall down. They do not leave one high and dry. They do not forget the most important component of any business. Salute in passing oh colleague. Do not fear. One's hopes and dreams will not fall on stony ground.

It does not matter how gifted the scientists are, how advanced the products, if those cannot be sold they will sit there in the warehouse. These are not planks of wood and tons of gravel. Wood and gravel will be of use in a thousand years' time. For new technologies all it takes is six months, if these cannot be sold in six months let them be consigned to the heap of forgotten ideas.

On a daily basis fevered spasms struck my brain. A customer said to me: William, your brains are palpitating, look! See the sides of your head: your temples are banging together. Look, look at your whatyacallthems!

How does one spell 'forever'?

The new technologies are of a certain order. Technologies do not change things in the world they change the world.

I had a proposal for Anne; not wedlock, of slightly greater importance than that. But she, however, was a woman.

What do I mean by that?

Nought may be taken for granted.

I had one ex-wife and one who – well, the reality, I had been a widower when I married her. My ex-wife was my second wife, My first wife died a heck of a long time ago. So so long ago. Mother of my daughter. Yes I thought of her. Parents, mothers, fathers.

It would be wrong to say that I did not think of her. Yes, I did, after so many years. I no longer felt like her lover because I had been her lover. I carried a photograph of her and had scanned a couple too. My daughter kept most of the photographs. She was quite remarkable really. She had a smile – what would one call it? – beautiful, the most beautiful smile. Girls are so damn open, they are so damn generous! In fact

move on.

Women regard wedlock in a favourable light.

Vodka and water. A typical drink. Not my favourite. A colleague described it as a 'working drink'.

Things that are truths are no longer truths. This type of mental whatdyacallit peregrination. By the time one remembers the context one has forgotten the word. It was age. Ten years ago I would have followed the thought, wrestled from it the sense. My line of work destroys the intellect. I was a university graduate. Now look at me. I glanced round quickly, having spoken aloud. I did. I thought I did anyway, maybe I did not, maybe it was

oh well, and if I had, what odds, what odds.

The reader of the quality newspaper appeared to be concentrating unduly. He must have heard me speak.

The reference was freedom. I saw it as a possibility, as substance. When I was a student, many years ago, I lived my life taking freedom for granted, intellectual freedom. Enmeshed in that assumption is the concept 'progress'. Students assume progress as a natural state. A false assumption. Nor, if it does exist, need it be chronological or should I say linear, geometrical rather than algebraic, in keeping with the digital thingwi, revolution.

Vodka and water.

Once a widower always a widower. If one's wife was one's first, one's first love. Not just a relationship, a marriage, complete with child, finished. One wee girl. It was nice having a wee girl.

It was a pleasant drink aside from anything. In the past I used cola which had become too sweet so then lemon, bitter lemon, stressing the bitter. A vodka and lemon please, bitter. Vodka and orange, bitter orange. Gin and bitter orange. Gin and lemon of course. But not gin and water. Why! And of course Spanish brandy and water, I had a fondness for Spanish brandy, if only to annoy the purists.

Drinks that do not stain the breath; which does not refer to the Spanish although it too renders one too eh well now how to say it, pissed.

Life is strange. Context is all. Without context where would we be? Where would the world be? This question is the most real. One might consider much. But, howsomever. Then when the context is human, a personned-entity, another person, i.e. not oneself. When another intellectual being, repository of humanned data, has become the context. Love is indicated.

How does one define love? Anne is not at all in the image of my first wife and yet and yet, needless to state, I, well, perhaps, ah, perhaps, indeed, may I love her, do I love her? do I do I – a song by Blossom Dearie, oh Anne do I love you, do I do I.

essence of woman

Language turns a man inside out. The world through Anne-tinted spectacles; today William is wearing his Anne-tints.

Having said all of that, ignoring reports and briefcases, if not for university I would not have read and appreciated Monsieur Sartre. I did appreciate Sartre. People condemn universities. Not me.

I was so looking forward to seeing her. I had failed to appreciate how much. If she was not going to turn up, and let us face it

Why was she not here? She was not here. She was not coming. Ha ha.

I was not a man for the one-liner. I enjoyed proper jokes. More jape than joke, and japer than joker. I performed japes. Allez oop. Just sign there madam.

Yet when it came to it, thinking about how much time I gave to her, to thoughts of her. Not all that much. I thought about everything else. But she was never faraway, lurked within, inside of the brain old gel, she was at the root, her presence determining negative space. Mine was the most healthy negative space one could discover: so much so it was the opposite of negativity where negativity is an unpositive element. Anne was the direct opposite, and inside my head she was like that. My head had been full of vile bitterness, a composition of bitterness and anger. And rage, irritation and frustration and bloody hurt sensitivity, hurt sensitivity, too much even to think about; such that it drove a man to distraction. Soon she would enter the bar. She would place her hand upon my brow. In a former life she was a healer. Upon the brows of the ill and dying, and they did heal. She has retained this ability through various transmigratory peregrinations. Peregrinations, a damn fine word. I would to construct a monument to my love, this woman of the balm. Vodka and water. I gestured with the glass as in a quiet salute to the dearly departed, the yet-to-arrive.

A bar worker was gazing across. I nodded to him but my nod was not acknowledged.

I was an interloper.

People's lives are sacred.

Through the side window the street lights blinked. It was early December yet still warm. I liked the north of England and Lancashire in particular. Jokes abounded but I found it okay. It was not dull and it was not dreary. Ever stepped down from Wigan Central and not enjoyed a large brandy in the bar of the Station Hotel? Or am I thinking of Rochdale? The old Station Bar had gone of course, like community fellowship, the days of which too had gone, yea. One crosses the road to the licensed grocer as once we termed the mini-market, a half bottle and a couple of cans for the rest of the trip home, perchance one avoids the more obvious error, madly dashing back up the stairs into the station and stumbling onto the slow train to Fleetwood, or Blackpool or where was I when the conductor came calling? Never mind sir.

It was two and a half hours since the text. Anne was most overdue, let us say – albeit her life, her life was complicated.

Other than Anne and my first wife I have had five women as serious presences in my own life, excluding my paternal grandmother with whom I had an early bond. My ex second wife, my present partner, my elderly mother, my daughter and Joan Richmond with whom I had a lengthy affair some years ago. It struck me that these six women, in fact seven – eight including my grandmother – shared characteristics yet nevertheless were so different.

In fact it was eight women. Dear god!

This was predictable.

Eight women.

My daughter did not count being of myself. I was attracted to aspects of myself. Yet at the same time we two were so different! How could we be so different and at the same time be aspects of the one?

Shared characteristics and traits. Such a cliche to say that I loved most all but I did, nevertheless, I did. I do not hesitate to use the word, 'love', for what is love? The indefinable, he said with a cheery grin. But Joan Richmond? I could not have loved Joan. Joan was just

I set down the new vodka and water, what was left of it, very little.

My ex second wife was generous.

My God almighty sometimes it took her ages, bloody ages, we are talking ages. If somebody said to me are you coming and I said yes I would be there in two minutes, but that did not work with one's spouse. Nor did it work with Anne. If she said two minutes it was two damn days by the time she took care of everything so I had to advance her notice beyond reasonable limits. But of course. What was wrong with that? People cannot be expected to drop everything. Especially women; which is no sexist joke. I do not like sexist jokes. Women require greater segments of space and time.

Hells bells.

The shifty looking smoker had returned to his seat and the door opening again. Whoopee. I was onto my feet and to her, grinning like a madman, taking her by the elbow. Anne Anne Anne. Sorry I'm late, she said.

Oh God, dont worry dont worry. I was laughing now and trying to put the reins on it. I showed her to where I was sitting, assuming she would sit on the chair next to me but she pulled back another, to sit facing me. I waited for her to talk. It was important to do so.

She looked so great. She did! She glanced about the room. Same old place, I said.

She grinned.

Oh jees. You are looking wonderful my dear, my god you are, you are, you truly are.

Anne whispered but too low and I couldnt hear. I asked her to please whisper it louder, more loudly.

I couldnt get away, she said quietly, self consciously. She gazed to the bar and added, You look tired.

I am. I'm going nuts into the bargain: g & t?

Thanks.

Imagine forgetting the damn drink!

I ordered another vodka and water for myself, a packet of crisps and a packet of nuts. I was looking forward to the night, looking forward to a meal. Where would we go? I hoped she would opt for Indian food. She preferred Chinese or Italian. I preferred Mexican or Indian. Grub needed bite. One for the notebook that. I smiled and shook my head. Grub needs bite, I said to the bar worker who didnt reply but smiled vaguely which is always fine by me; if I get somebody to smile then half the battle be o'er, I shall get them to buy, for 'tis my job, the modus operandi.

Anne was signalling to me; munch munch. She was wanting a packet of crisps!

Allez oop. I abracadabrad at the bar where lay the bag of crisps side by side with the the bag of nuts. The bar worker smiled honestly while handing me my change. Thank you most kindly, I said.

Anne ate her crisps in a mechanical way. But it was interesting. I was chomping a nut. Nuts for me and crisps for her. Aha! Hey! I said, a wee test.

She chuckled, and it stopped me in my tracks. I had been about to say something but her chuckle, her chuckle. You're laughing at me, I said.

Wee test...! She shook her head, smiling.

My Scotteesh voice senorita eet knock you for seex? Seriously, I said and I snatched the packet of crisps out her hand. Without looking at the packet, what flavour's the crisps?

What do you mean?

Nothing, I'm just asking.

Could you repeat it?

What flavour's the crisps?

Aah... Anne frowned for a moment, then studied me. I know it's a trick.

It's not, I said.

Mm. She frowned again. Is flavours a noun or a verb?

Pardon...

Is flavours a noun or a verb? she asked.

I looked at her. She was smiling at me. Anne smiled at me. Her hand was to her mouth, and she reached for my hand and held it, she studied it, turning it palm up, examining it for personality indicators or signs of the future. When do you go away? she said.

Tomorrow evening.

Are you working tomorrow?

I've got to be.

She nodded, she now was holding my hand with both of hers; both of her hands, she kind of cradled mine. My hand. What was I? Just a damn man.

That's why you're here, she said.

I couldnt reply. I was the best part of I think what is thunderstruck because this is what I was and felt like crying and felt as if I could cry right there. The whole of life was too good to be true and I was the luckiest man in the whole world and that is the God's truth so help me my Lord God, the one bright star in the dismal night sky. She was the only only thing. She pushed aside the crisps and studied her drink. She raised her head to look at me but only for a moment.

What's wrong? I said.

She smiled but kept her head lowered. You are always so sharp, she said.

I saw the worry in her. My hand went to hers, rested on it. It was above her nose where the worry was, in line with her eyebrows. I wanted to stroke there, easing it, the burden there. I glanced at the empty seat beside me. Come round here, I said, please. Come round here: sit beside me. She shook her head and continued studying my hand, which I made to withdraw, it was strange to me at this moment. I shifted on the seat, edgily, although there was nothing wrong. If anyone had asked me, nothing.

Such Grace, The Thief

Mark Buckland

The night the firework factory blew up, I accidentally killed my brother for the fourth time. I was stood at the kitchen window, watching the fire, when it burst and turned the street to clouds of pepper. I'd been watching for an hour while cleaning dishes, lathering every item till I just about took the pattern from the plates. It was hypnotic. Dark plumes with starlight inside. Then the blast and I jumped. I didn't hear Michael behind me and before I knew it, I'd stuck a soapy knife in his chest.

'Oh, fuck. I'm really sorry, Mikey,' I said. He dropped onto his back.

He lay on the floor, a second mouth open in the middle of his torso. 'It's fine. Just leave me a minute,' he choked, blood peeping at his mouth.

Behind us, the uninvited Hogmanay was going on. I stepped over him and went into the living room. I sat in front of the TV and scanned the channels for something about the fire. Out the window there, I could see strobing silhouettes of firemen, forty feet high against the remains of the factory wall. I heard Michael croak next door and then there was silence. He was dead. About ten minutes later, he strode through and sat on the other couch. He lit a cigarette and looked out at the scene outside.

'Mikey, mate, I'm really sorry, I just got spooked by the fireworks.'

'Aye,' he replied, dragging, 'it's fine.'

The wound was gone and he had that groggy look he always has after he's died.

When Michael was nine, our mother killed him for his second time, her first. Accident, you understand. She slapped him across the head as we were walking out of the high flats, he stumbled down both sets of stairs and continued his waggling run into the road. A 4x4 met him dead on and crumpled him to bad origami. My mother, already lugging a pram in one hand, became a white pillar. I ran over to Michael and stood with the driver, who was shrieking. She was definitely not from the scheme, probably back from the school run. She had on this expensive jacket which she took off to cover him. She hovered over Michael, holding it, debating whether to ruin the coat. She looked like a matador fighting a bull that had spontaneously combusted.

Then he moved.

I jumped down beside him and in my best 4 year old words, tried to talk to him. I tried to say goodbye, I suppose. I remember how I felt the first time. I didn't want my mother to feel like that. This time; this weird, sedate calm was on me. Then Michael's right hand, which had gone back to front, turned around and crunched. 'A'm awright, Willie,' he gurgled, his face, an over-boiling pot. And then he sat up.

'Here,' he said, lighting another smoke and putting his feet up on the couch. 'you goin' tae the game this weekend?'

'No,' I said. 'Mikey, like I said mate, I'm really sorry. A really am.' My original accent always migrates back to me when I'm around him.

'How no?'

'Cash, Mikey.'

'Is it cause ae me?'

'Naw, you know it's no.'

That second time, Michael was fully recovered by the time the ambulance got there. He was walking. The driver had wrapped him in her coat eventually. Every broken bone was healed, the seam that had opened on the back of his head had stitched itself up. He was just a bloodied t-shirt, like a bad Halloween costume.

The doctors spent an age with him alone. My maw was distraught, she just twitched back and forth in the waiting room. Then we got to see him. He was eating ice cream and I remember being jealous of that. We were listening to the doctor explain that Michael's bones had completely reset, as if nothing had happened, when a nurse came in and handed a folder to that white coat. He stopped talking and my mother started shaking again. She took out her cigarettes and placed one in her mouth; the doctor looked up: 'You can't smoke in here.'

'A canny?'

'No. This has happened before, I see,' pointing to the folder. The first time. My accident. The inexplicable.

After that, it was weeks of tests. He got to be off school, so we were at home a lot together. Battering each other. Maw slapping us back into peace.

Then there were lots of home visits. My maw just sat in the corner when they did, smoking, watching Michael. She was a wee bit afraid of him, I think.

A large explosion shook the whole room. I flinched and Michael just changed the channel over to that quiz show he likes.

'Here, Willie, fire down the shoaps fur us, aye? Get us a bag of crisps and some ginger.'

'I don't think I can the now mate, no wae all that going on ootside.'

'It's in Minnesota, ya arsehole,' he shouted. I felt myself recoil, before I realised it was the TV he was talking to.

That's the thing – Michael has always been smart. The doctors and social workers, even the government when they got involved, said so. A very intelligent young boy who just happens to be immortal. They found that out after about a year. Michael could regenerate at a cellular level, almost instantly. He was ageing, but not as fast as the rest of us. And then somebody let it all out to the press.

'Willie, A've goat a hell of a drouth oan. Get us some ginger.'

'Mikey, wait till all that's over out there.'

'Aw that?' He pointed to the kaleidoscope of death going on less than a mile away. 'That's nuthin.'

THE MIRACLE BOY. That was when I knew it would be different. My maw still has that newspaper somewhere in her big book. An archive, if you like. We were on a chat show. 'Can I touch you?' the glossy woman presenter said to Michael. Full of awe, she was. Bright eyed. 'Aye, whitever,' Michael had said. I realised, even then, how posh he made the presenter sound. She reached out to grab his arm and I don't know why I said it, but I shouted out 'it's my birthday next week.' I've watched the VHS of it back; my toes curl every time. What I actually wanted to do was grab this red-top hag and tell her not to touch my big brother. I didn't know why, but it became clearer later.

'That's nothing to you, Mikey. It's a hazard to the rest of us.'

'Hazard. Wrap that patter.'

He got up and walked over to the window. He observed the hazard.

'Place looks fuckin' mental.' He stubbed his cigarette out on his palm, an old party trick people used to love.

There was the tour of America. Big fancy hotels, each room the size of our flat, although it wasn't the council flat for us when we got back. Papers, more chat shows. I had an argument with my maw before we went on one, something about a toy shop, and she called me a 'bad wee cunt' on *The Montel Williams show*. The whole audience was going to have a stroke. The fat woman in the front row tipped over like the Hindenburg.

'Here, Willie, wis that always a firework factory?'

'Aye.'

'Wilnae be now.'

'Nope.'

My maw, in the paper, a year in. MIRACLE BOY'S MONSTER MUM. *Her*, looking into camera, *outside our flat, skelping my backside with a fist. Her hair roots were showing, brown through blonde.* When I look back, she looked tired. *Meghan Armstrong, a single mother, smokes and drinks before BEATING HER SONS: Miracle Boy Michael, 11, and his brother, William, 7.*

And his brother, William, 28. Looking at Michael as he bangs his head on the glass, to an unheard hardcore rhythm. He let his forehead slide down, streaking the window. I knew what he was thinking. I knew what he had seen while he was dead, this time around. With his eyes, he would see the firemen. Magenta, orange, blue; a human rainbow.

After a while, the media lost interest. An immortal wean is only good for a short season of column inches, especially after you've picked apart his maw's failings, dug up an old auntie we didn't remember and reunited him with his da. That's when I think I noticed it. I was young but I could see it. Ma da, smiling, arm around a stony faced Miracle Boy. *I'm going to try and patch things up with his mother*, read one part of the interview. And that's all you need when you're wee – a hint that things might get better. You soon grow out of that.

'Willie, anyhin' you want tae tell me?'

'Sit doon mate, tonnes tae talk about.'

Miracle Boy was 18 and I was 14 and we were going to parties; empties, whose maw was oot fur the night. And he was a big thing. He could drink the house dry and not need a stomach pump. He would drink bleach and lie on someone's living room floor, spraying white foam like a hot spring.Everyone cheered. Then, slowly, he hated it. He still looked 12 and birds laughed at him. He became the joke. People would phone me and say if I was coming out, don't bring your brother, *that wee freaky prick*. Kids would box him at school, just for the craic. Blades in the ribs, all of that. He just took it, till whatever wannabe hardman had punched himself out.

Then one day, some teacher called him *Miracle Boy*, like any day, and he put a desk into the man's chest. Photographers back at the door, the new suburban PVC door. The world's press, reporting live in Glasgow, on an injury to a supply geography teacher.

Then he started calling himself *Michael Lazarus*. And he didn't want to die anymore. Both things, the papers ignored. I didn't. He wanted to be called that for a reason, but it wasn't clear at first. Goth phase? He had started hanging around some of the middle-class folk where we lived now. One time, he was showing off to some girls by slicing his neck. They hated it; one threw up. *Ewww, boggin*. After he had been under, he went and said to Big Dee that he shouldn't ride motorbikes anymore. The reply was just a laugh and a ruffle of the immortal hair, a titty-twister of the everliving nipple. A week later and three feet of Big Dee was in a tree and the remaining three feet was still on a bike.

And I asked him then. 'I get a foreshadow,' he said. And I thought that was the most syllables he'd ever used in a word, so he must mean it. That was me in my teens, knowing what he meant. And he knew that I understood and that I understood the gap between us.

There was a loud bang, then a delay before all the windows exploded. I ducked to the floor, Michael just stood in front of the spray of glass like it was a snowstorm. From outside, there were shouts. I looked up and Michael lit another cigarette and strolled back to the couch. His face was war-painted with lacerations. He looked like a pizza in motion.

'Jesus. What happened?'

'Hefty badafuckinboom,' he said, letting the new breeze wash over him. Smoke was wafting in, finding new air to explore.

And then it all came out. It all poured out of me in the exactly the way I didn't want to do it.

'There's firemen fighting out there! You could do something, get out there and do something!'

'Five of them just died,' he replied.

What he saw when he was under, this latest time.

Every time Michael Lazarus went under he could see something of the future, like a dream you never wanted making room in your morning thoughts. And then he came back Mikey.

'Then what the fuck are you doing? Get out there, you could put this out in ten minutes.'

'No ma joab,' he said.

You have to understand, I didn't want to have this conversation and not in this way, I'd spent the whole evening shunpiking it, choking buckets with him, watching reruns of *Who Wants To Be A Millionaire*, anything. A man from the government came to see me. We'd met before, back when Michael went on the dole. 'A'm movin' back near hame mate,' he had announced. To him, the leafy detatched estate with the 4x4's haunting the drives was the same as the tower block estate with nae cars ootside. 'A'd rather no talk tae cunts like me than no talk tae cunts who arnae like me.' That, I couldn't disagree with him oan. If you wanted silence and isolation, better to do it among yer ain than among Waitrose-worriers.

But the government guy was more pressing these days. The thought of paying housing benefit for the next ten thousand years probably spooked them a wee bit.

I picked my way across the glass. 'Michael, please mate, go and do this.'

'Naw.' He smoked.

'Mr Armstrong, I hope you can understand that there are some very... difficult debates being had in parliamentary groups right now?'

'Difficult how?'

'Difficult in ethics.'

I knew what he meant. Michael Lazarus goes to work. Either that or someone finds a way to *really* kill him. They didn't know the clairvoyant thing, that was still a card we could play. MIRACLE BOY SAVES TEN THOUSAND TROOPS WITH VISION OF FUTURE TO COME. That's how I thought it might work. The journos could find a snappier headline. We'd have no shortage of a war for Michael to strategise on.

'Mikey, look at what's happening out there. You could save lives. You could do something, fuck, I don't care if you want to go back to selling beauty products—'

Miracle Cream. For Those Who Live Forever. His face on the billboards.

'—but you're no good to anybody in here.'

'What A'd really like,' he started saying, 'is a tub of ice cream.'

Michael the Miracle. Michael, who couldn't get off benefits. The immortal man who lived in a one bed flat in Pollokshaws, two down from where he grew up, which he hadn't left for ten years, other than a Thursday trip to the Post Office.

'Mind that stuff you used to get at Millport, Willie? No the Whippy shite. The mad tub ae the thingy family. That. A'd heavy like that the now.'

I took a 30secs panic attack and looked around the living room, what was left of it. Then I just looked at the floor. My lungs were filling up, that aluminium taste aniseeding my mouth. Then I looked at Michael and I saw it, for the first time.

I thought I knew what it was. I went to university; Michael couldn't, too much attention on him. I changed. I turned maw into mother and turned that into an occasional Christmas card. I turned a girl's womb into a foetus and then into William Jr, wee Wulyam. I'd travelled all over the world, he could barely take a trip to the high-rise's lift. Michael hadn't done any of that, couldn't do any of that – that's what I thought it was about. But it wasn't.

The cuts on Michael's face were already scars. Soon they would be skin again. He took a long drag. His lungs would blacken and then puff back to pink, like cherry blossom follows winter.

'His presence in the world has created a range of religious debate, Mr Armstrong. Many are discussing an end to his life.'

Michael got up and tapped the broken TV, trying to revive it.

'Encased in concrete or acid is the favoured idea at the moment.'

They didn't know that he still felt pain. They just assumed he didn't.

'That's that fucked then,' he sighed.

I saw it in him, every day. He could see the future. He couldn't die. And after I was dead, after our maw was dead, after all the reporters who chased him, all the politicians who were scared of him – after they all had passed, it would still be him. After the world was over, Michael would be sitting on the wreckage. Smoking and trying to remember the name of that Millport ice cream.

A fireman appeared where the window once was, floating on a cherry picker. He was oily and stained like an ashtray.

'Yez need tae leave right noo, this is gonnae get wurse. Why huv yez no evacuatit?' he said.

The first accident, you're probably wondering. We were playing in the park and I pushed Michael. He's my big brother. I'm 3, I don't expect him to fall. His foot wrung all the impending danger out of a tree root and he went in the river.

'We will, sir, thank you. How are you guys getting on out there?' I nodded, as if it was the most normal thing, to be addressed by a fireman at your brother's blown out window, fourteen floors up.

He fell in the river. He was swept away fast. I watched him, thrashing arms, like unwelcome fins. And I saw his eyes as he went over the falls. My mother's scream. The eyes, though. He was scared, really scared, back then. The world could do something to him to harm him and he knew it.

'No so good pal, might spread tae that factory behind,' the fireman said. 'Ye's gonnae get tae then?'

'Naw,' said Michael. He took another draw of his cigarette and took his phone out. 'Naw, A'm good where A am.'

Sugar Cake Trail

Christina Neuwirth

I have bought a sugar cake for her and a sugar cake for me. The bag is flimsy and I scrunch the top up and swing it around, around. We walk between buildings to the promenade, and the sunny day comes out to look at us. It is early, so in the shade I get a little chill, but the sun soon warms me up all the way. The smell of fresh bread wafts up to us through the vents in the basements of the bakeries. My face stings where I put the aftershave, and it feels sticky and smooth in the breeze. Her hair is long and streaked with blonde from the summer by the lake.

When we kiss she will taste grainy and of water lilies, but that comes later. Not on the first day. Not like that.

I leave a sugartrail.

Margaret is holding her jumper in one hand, its sleeves brushing the ground. She doesn't appear to mind. Her shoulders have freckles on them and her arms are smooth and always moving when she talks. She is a little bit shorter than me, so when I stand close by I can see her thick fringe but not her eyes, except when she tilts her head up.

When she agreed to meet I was surprised she suggested such an early time. 10am is very early. It made me think, wow, she really wants to spend a day with me. We will meet at 10 and then we will forget the time and all of a sudden it'll be late in the evening and we'll have forgotten to eat, and then we'll get hot dogs from the last stall that's open on the town square, and we'll eat it by the fountain and the bench will be warm with the heat of the day. And when we eat the hot dogs we'll feel safe in our silence, because we'll have talked all day.

Margaret and I walk the promenade by the lake. The trees are evenly spaced out and it's early enough in the day to find a bench to sit down on. Each time we get close to one I unclench my grasp on the paper bag full of sugar cakes, but we only slow down a little bit and then decide we're not really tired at all. No need to sit. Just keep walking. The shops on our left are sleepily opening their doors, sixteen-year-olds heaving signposts advertising ice cream, swimsuits and lemonade.

I leave a sugartrail.

The sugar cakes are special cakes for carnival. I bought them at the bakery right before I met her, and they made it awkward to hug her to say hello, the bag hanging limply on the side.

Margaret takes hold of her jumper before we sit down and ties it around her waist, ties a big knot. We sit down in a patch of grass underneath a tree. The lake spreads out in front of us and tickles the bottoms of the mountains. Finally I let go of the paper bag and give her one of the cakes and bite into one myself. Powdered sugar all over her nose and chin, apricot jam on her bottom lip. She laughs and slaps her bare knee when I point it out, then takes a handkerchief and wipes her face clean, but still sticky. I am transfixed by the red mark she has left on her skin, and the scrunched-up piece of cloth in the long grass. She likes the cake.

'This is Margaret,' I say when I introduce her to the friend we bump into, by the lake, blinking into the sun. He raises his eyebrow and I blush right up to my eyelids.

It's the first time I've said her name out loud to anyone else. I don't yet know what variations I will find for it, the times I will say it in anger, the times she will say it as she picks up the phone and how it will mold to the mouths of our children.

When we are on a boat her hair sticks to where the jam was. It whips all around her face and blows into my eyes. The lake is a quiet, sleek mirror. We stand on the deck as long as we can stand it and shout our conversation back and forth. I point out parts of the landscape. She points out other parts.

When it gets too windy and cold and my ears feel like they might fall off, we head into the belly of the boat to the little café. We drink a cup of coffee. It is bitter, but I drink it black. Margaret doesn't notice. She talks with both of her hands even when she's holding the cup of coffee.

I tell her my prepared story about traffic, the one where I get fake-irate only to reveal I was on a bus all along. She smiles.

I wonder if we'll ever go on a bus together, maybe when we're retired. I'll pack lunch for us and she will fall asleep on my shoulder after we pass the border. We will take the bus all the way to a green beach in Slovenia. We will see two seagulls tearing apart a pigeon and hurry back to the bungalow to make love hard and fast, to erase the image. She will cycle down the dusty dirt road in the morning to buy milk in cold glass bottles from the grocer's by the church. Her legs will be wrinkly, but lean and tanned. Ferrets will crouch in the corners of our terrace while we eat bread and honey.

We sit on the pier and she takes off her shoes. Her pale feet dangle in the breeze, her toes long like twigs.

In the winter we will go to the mountains and those toes will get cold and white, and I'll warm them in between my knees in bed after a long day of skiing. When she's warmed up again we'll go to the cabin's kitchen and the cook will make an omelet with fried dumplings in it, soft egg around the edges, pumpkin seed oil over it, and we'll eat it with chunks of bread torn off a fresh loaf. The oil will glisten like a malachite, green and black, and it will dribble down my chin where she will wipe it off with her napkin.

I leave a sugartrail.

After the boat ride she is cold. She unties the big knot on her belly and puts her jumper back on. She's still cold. I didn't bring a jacket because I was expecting the weather to be on my side. I offer to buy her a scarf, and she laughs and gets angry with me, but only for a little while. We do go into a shop and she sees a scarf that she likes, but we walk out without buying anything. She's very quiet.

I ask, 'Are you tired?'

She says, 'Yes. I suppose we could take a seat.'

I can suggest a place to eat, but we had sugar cakes only a little while ago. We sit on a bench and look at the lake again.

We will find a lovely restaurant near our flat and the staff will know the names of our children. They will serve us cold cuts of meat in vinegary marinade with big tough beans named for beetles. Smoked ham, flaky, with gherkins, tiny gherkins cut like a fan. Horseradish on a board on the side, a whole root, and I will grate it a little bit at a time. We will cut the bread into soldiers and dip it into smooth beige mustard to make the horseradish stick, but no horseradish for the children, it's too strong for them, but the little one, Anna, will ask to try some because she will be brave. It'll go right up her nose, that heat, and Margaret will hand her a slice of bread to smell because the smell of bread eases the pain.

She shakes her head and says she's got to be on her way home.

We will see a play while Christoph and Anna are away to learn how to play tennis. Margaret will put on perfume after she has washed off the smell of the day from her back, and the smell of the hospital from her hands. And she will wear her favourite dress and pin her grandmother's brooch on it, the one with the daisies made from enamel and gold. It will be a special night, and we will get a taxi to the theatre. Our seats won't be the best but we won't mind because the actors enunciate so well that we don't miss a word. And after the play we will have a glass of champagne at the bar of the theatre, and it will be expensive but it'll be okay because it's a very special night and we're treating ourselves, for once.

I say, 'That's a shame, I was hoping we could spend a little more time together. I'm starving! Are you sure you don't want to go for a bite to eat? The pub around the corner does a great goulash soup, and they serve warm rolls with it and you don't even have to pay extra for the rolls. Goulash soup needs rolls, to dunk into it, you know.'

She nods. She knows.

'I'd love to but I'm awfully tired and I'd really best just head home.'

We leave a sugartrail.

Margaret will boil plum dumplings on Mondays because they're Christoph's favourite. She will make the cheese dough and wrap it around the cold plums straight from the fridge while the salty water boils on the stove. Then she will cook them and make sweet cinnamon breadcrumbs turned in butter in a metal pan. The kids will watch TV on the floor and I will set the table, flat big plates and a knife and fork and a spoon, even though we know we'll only use the spoon. They will be soft, and the spoon will cut into the hot plums, and their juice will stain the breadcrumbs purple. Christoph will like plum dumplings all the way until he hits puberty and grows a small smudge of a moustache, when he suddenly claims he never liked them, because he will get it into his head that boys don't like sweet things, and I will slap him for talking back to his mother.

She apologises again and turns around, hugging her arms to her chest for warmth. I kick myself for not insisting on getting her the scarf. Then she remembers something and comes back and embraces me lightly, quickly.

'Goodbye! Thanks for the boat ride!'

'I hope you had a nice time.'

'I had a nice time.'

'Get home safely!'

'I will. I'll call you.'

We will light a fire in the garden for Easter, when we buy a house. It will be a small fire because you're not really supposed to light fires in your gardens. The kids will toast corn on the cob and I will slice butter to rub on it, and there will be a bowl of salt and pepper. Their faces will be greasy. Margaret will eat cherries and watch the smoke go up towards the sky, and I will sit behind her and bury my face in her hair, all the way in, until my nose hits her freckled shoulder.

I finally throw out the bag from the bakery. I think about meeting some friends for a drink, but I go home instead.

She doesn't call.

The summer ends.

Elegy for a Makar

Olga Wojtas

Letter from Isla Maciver to Donald Maciver

My Dear Donald

Campbell is growing weaker by the day – my tears could burn through cold steel, such is my grief at seeing what this great man has become. But he is proud, so very proud – he cannot bear others to see his dreadful frailty, and I am the only one he will have beside him. I beg you, tell his dear friends that they should now stop trying to contact him, since it distresses him beyond measure. Let them remember him as he was.

I give you leave to show them this letter.

Love from Aunt Isla

Letter from Isla Maciver to Donald Maciver

My Dear Donald

A very great shock today – Chris Grieve and Valda turned up on the doorstep, determined to see Campbell. Thankfully, he did not hear them arrive and I managed to get rid of them. But you really must make it plain that we are not to be disturbed; this is in your interest as well as mine. I have disconnected the phone, to avoid incoming calls and in case Campbell might take it into his head to ring someone, though he shows no inclination to do anything but write – I can scarcely keep up the work of transcription.

Love from Aunt Isla

Letter from Isla Maciver to Donald Maciver

My Dear Donald

It is a terrible, terrible thing that has been done, and soon I must stand before the Judgment Seat and accept what is due to me. But the truth must also be known among the living also, so once I have been committed to the ground, I wish you to make full disclosure.

My love, my thanks, my pity,

Aunt Isla

a.l.hunter@ed.ac.uk to DomhnallMac@gmail.com

Dear Mr Maciver

I hope you don't mind me contacting you – I got your email address from the Scottish Book Trust. My name is Angela Hunter and I've recently successfully completed a PhD on Isla Maciver at Edinburgh University, where I now have a Leverhulme Early Career Fellowship.

My mother used to recite *The Hecklebirnie Randan* to me when I was a wee girl, although it was a long time before I discovered what it was really about! It was reading Maciver's *Elegy for a Makar* which decided me to study Scottish literature. Edinburgh University Press has been very encouraging about my expanding my thesis into a book, and I would be extremely grateful if it were possible to interview you about your late aunt. You can check my credentials on my university web page, www.humanities.ed.ac.uk/staff/angelahunter.

I look forward to hearing from you.

Kindest regards

Angela Hunter

DomhnallMac@gmail.com to a.l.hunter@ed.ac.uk

Dear Dr Hunter

Thank you for your email. I'm not sure how much help I can be to you. I handed over all the material I had from her, correspondence, manuscripts, and so on, to her literary executor and, as you will know, all of these papers have been deposited in the National Library. You will also know that I have been interviewed a number of times about Isla and I don't know what more I can add. But let me not dampen your enthusiasm for what sounds an admirable project. Might I suggest meeting at the Cafe Royal on Tuesday at 5pm?

Best wishes

Donald Maciver

a.l.hunter@ed.ac.uk to DomhnallMac@gmail.com

Dear Mr Maciver

Thank you so much for a lovely evening! I had assumed we would only have a quick drink, and it was incredibly kind of you to extend it to dinner. I enjoyed your company tremendously, and not just because of the conversation about Isla. Would you consider letting me return the favour, and come round to my flat for dinner? Friday evening around 7pm? My address is 16 Marchmont Road, first floor right. Please let me know if that would suit you.

Thank you again,

Angela

DomhnallMac@gmail.com to a.l.hunter@ed.ac.uk

Dear Angela (if I may)

There is absolutely no favour to be returned – I too very much enjoyed your company. But if you're sure I'm not putting you to too much trouble, I would be delighted to come round on Friday evening. Please allow me to bring the wine.

I look forward to seeing you then,

Donald

a.l.hunter@ed.ac.uk to DomhnallMac@gmail.com

Dear Donald

Yesterday evening was wonderful, and I really hope I didn't offend you when you were leaving. Although I had been drinking the very excellent wine you brought, I wasn't at all drunk, and knew exactly what I was doing. I have to tell you that I find you extremely attractive, and the impulse to kiss you was simply too strong. I'm very afraid I've spoiled things between us. But I would very much like to see you again.

Angela

DomhnallMac@gmail.com to a.l.hunter@ed.ac.uk

My dear Angela

What a delightful email to receive! When one is at such an advanced age as myself, one assumes that the only reason for a kiss from a charming young lady would be complete intoxication!

I would very much like to see you again. But I'm afraid my culinary skills are non-existent so, much as I would like to invite to you dine at my home, I'm afraid it will have to be elsewhere. May I suggest the Scotch Malt Whisky Society in Queen Street? And if it's not too soon, tomorrow evening?

Donald

DomhnallMac@gmail.com to J.S.Scott@talktalk.co.uk

Jim

You're not answering your phone so I presume you're still locked up in the library. It was only the other day, I recall, that you remarked our best days were behind us. You owe me a large Glenfiddich. A sonsie wee lassie has just kissed me full on the lips, told me she finds me extremely attractive and that she wants to see me again. Ach, the Maciver charm is eternal. She's a bright wee girl too, at the start of her academic career, and not bad-looking.

Let me know when you're buying me that drink, but not tomorrow night – other plans!

Donald

angie@madasafish.com to Barbara.Grant@blueyonder.co.uk

Hi Barbara

I have An Admirer! He's quite a noted figure on the literary scene, but since you're a complete philistine, you'll never have heard of him. His name's Donald Maciver, and he's the nephew of Scotland's most famous modern poet, Isla Maciver. Yes, the one I wrote my PhD on. It's obvious from her letters that she was very fond of him. No, not like that – she was the bidie-in of Campbell Dalrymple. Campbell Dalrymple, dear, Scotland's most famous modern poet before Isla – oh, never mind...

Anyway, Donald's never really spoken about her. But then, he's never spoken to me before. He's the most appalling old letch, sits there with his tongue hanging out, staring down my cleavage. How are you getting on with your crystallography? White coat decently buttoned up to the neck, I hope. Fancy going to a film next weekend?

Cheers,

Angie

a.l.hunter@ed.ac.uk to DomhnallMac@gmail.com

Dear Donald

I'm mortified to be putting you to all this trouble and expense – but selfish enough to say yes in order to be able to spend another evening with you. But we *must* sort something out so that it will be my treat the next time!

Very much looking forward to seeing you tomorrow,

Angela

angie@madasafish.com to Barbara.Grant@blueyonder.co.uk

Hi Barbara

Really sorry, but going to have to cancel our cinema trip – got a hot date, eurghh. I'm spending the weekend with Mr M at his place, a mansion in Fairmilehead. Thankfully, it won't all be fun and games. He's a fanatical golfer, at which point I shall go into domestic goddess mode and make his tea. Honestly, the things we do for our careers. So can we make it a week on Saturday for the film?

Angie

DomhnallMac@gmail.com to J.S.Scott@talktalk.co.uk

Jim

Still at your incessant labour? Mine is set to be of an entirely more pleasurable kind – Clarinda hastens to her Sylvander and a consummation devoutly to be wished. No idea when I'll be free for that dram.

Donald

DomhnallMac@gmail.com to a.l.hunter@ed.ac.uk

My dear Angela

I know you said you would make your own way here, but I cannot bear the thought of such precious cargo being at the mercy of Lothian Regional Transport! It's also quite a hike up to the house, although the views of the Pentlands are worth it. Waitrose delivers the basic necessities to me every week (although I shall be ordering superior breakfast ingredients – Buck's Fizz and croissants!), so let me know what else you need, and I'll add that to the list.

Counting the hours,

Donald

a.l.hunter@ed.ac.uk to DomhnallMac@gmail.com

Dear Donald

You are so bad! I promised this was going to be my treat, so I certainly didn't expect you to get anything! But it would be incredibly kind of you to collect me, since the buses are utterly unpredictable. You are quite the loveliest man in the world.

Angela x

angie@madasafish.com to Barbara.Grant@blueyonder.co.uk

I HAVE HIT THE JACKPOT!!! I still can't believe it. And now I'm going to have to explain it to you in words of one syllable because you're a bloody scientist and you won't understand :o(

It's the research breakthrough of the millennium, like discovering potassium permanganate is really hydrochloric acid.

Just back from chez Donald. Fabulous house, full of the most incredible artworks, hundreds of first editions – you would have hated it, not a single test tube or Bunsen burner in sight. Anyway, let us not dwell on the time we spent together <shudder>Let us instead skip to the point when he went to meet his golfing buddies. My cunning plan had rather backfired, since he was so desperate to talk about 'us' (in his dreams!) that I couldn't get him to keep to the subject of Isla. You remember Isla? Scotland's most famous modern poet? So after he sodded off, I went on a wee wander round the house to see if there was anything of interest. Oh, and there was! A stack of letters from Isla to her nephew. Letters which I photographed with my fab wee Olympus and which are now on to my laptop.

And you remember Isla lived with Campbell Dalrymple, Scotland's greatest etc before her? He was much older than she was, and was seen as her mentor. She actually wasn't that brilliant a poet when she started. But she was devoted to him, and nursed him through his last illness in their wee but'n'ben at the back of beyond. After he died, she published the collection that made her name, *Elegy for a Makar*. People said it was as though she was channelling him. Nothing so paranormal, according to these letters. She'd bloody nicked his poems! She'd found out he was leaving his royalties to the National Library, not to her, so she decided they weren't going to get any more. Her devoted nursing consisted of keeping everybody well away from him so they didn't know that although he was feeble and bed-ridden, he was writing every minute that he could. And she had Donald in Edinburgh showing all the literati a letter from her saying Dalrymple was so ill and frail he didn't want to see them.

Once Dalrymple pegged it, she gathered all the poems to do with death, tweaked them a bit and presented them as hers. Those poems about loss and loneliness are just that wee bit more poignant when you know that Dalrymple, poor bugger, was wondering why none of his mates could be arsed to get in touch.

And he'd been so prolific, she still had loads to put into further collections. When people say she surpassed Dalrymple, what it actually means is that he wrote his greatest work on his deathbed.

And then on *her* deathbed, she came over all repentant and told Donald to tell everyone the bad thing she'd done. Which Mr 'I-handed-everything-over-to-her-literary-executor' signally failed to do. She'd kept him onside, btw, with some dosh from Campbell's estate and the promise of *her* royalties.

It's absolute dynamite! It will change Scottish literary studies for ever! I'm just soooo excited! I had to make an excuse and leave – hinted at mysterious gynaecological disorders, knowing he'd never dare inquire further. What a wanker, keeping the letters. Should have burned them. Btw, you'd better delete this...

Bit worried about how I can take it from here. Will have to ask Si.

See you soon – happy crystallising!

Angie

angie@madasafish.com to simonhunter45@mac.com
Hey Big Bro!
Seeking legal advice. (And only legal advice, no moralising.)
A researcher friend came across some correspondence in someone's house, which is crucially important for her work. She took photographs of the letters and left them where they were.
What she wants to know is:a) has she committed any sort of offence?; b) if she has, what penalty could she face?; and c) can she use this material in her research?
She needs to know asap. Grateful thanks in advance, and I owe you dinner.

Love you,
Angie

DomhnallMac@gmail.com to a.l.hunter@ed.ac.uk
Dearest Angela
I do hope you're feeling a little better now. I was desperately sorry you had to leave. Look after yourself, and get in touch when you can.
I'm here, waiting for you.
Love,
Donald

DomhnallMac@gmail.com to a.l.hunter@ed.ac.uk
Dearest Angela
Are you all right? I'm terribly concerned about you. You haven't answered any of my calls. I don't want to pester you if you're unwell, but I'm worried in case you might need my help.
Please get in touch.
Love,
Donald

a.l.hunter@ed.ac.uk to DomhnallMac@gmail.com

Sorry, frantically busy with teaching right now, and wrestling with a research proposal. Feeling fine, thanks.

Best,

Angela

DomhnallMac@gmail.com to a.l.hunter@ed.ac.uk

Angela

I am concerned to find that some of my private papers have been disarranged. No-one apart from yourself and my cleaning lady, whom I trust implicitly, has been in my home. I regret having to ask you this, but have you gone through letters of mine from Isla? I must point out to you that these are confidential.

Donald

DomhnallMac@gmail.com to a.l.hunter@ed.ac.uk

Angela

I am very disturbed not to have heard from you. I fear I must put the worst possible construction on your silence and assume that you have read my private correspondence. Let me spell out to you that should you attempt to capitalise on the information you have stolen, I shall have you prosecuted for theft. You will also be liable for punitive damages in regard to breach of copyright.

Donald Maciver

a.l.hunter@ed.ac.uk to DomhnallMac@gmail.com

Mr Maciver

I'm afraid your grasp of the law is somewhat shaky. Nobody broke into your house and nothing was removed from your house, therefore no theft has occurred. The issue of copyright in letters is complex, and it is highly questionable whether the copyright of letters written to you belongs to you. If you believed that anyone had breached copyright, you would, of course, have to raise a civil action which you would have to fund yourself, with no guarantee of recouping your costs.

You must also consider the content of the correspondence to which you refer. Is it, for example, intended for your eyes only, or did your correspondent wish it to reach a wider audience? If the latter, what is your justification for failing to pass on this material? Of course, I simply raise these questions hypothetically.

Dr Angela Hunter

DomhnallMac@gmail.com to J.S.Scott@talktalk.co.uk

Jim, been ringing but just getting your voicemail. Hoping you're accessing email. Come round as soon as you can. Bring a bottle of Glenfiddich.

The Beautiful Birds of the Aftermath

Helen McClory

From dawn, the birds were taken from their boxes and placed in a long row on the wall of the battery. Maree's job was to smooth out the feathers and check that all parts of the birds were still sturdily affixed. She had brought up a box of eyes and another of claws. The feathers were hard to get hold of; the town ordered in fresh skins and extras of the long filamentaries direct from Tasmania – these were expensive, but the budget allowed for the cost, and if there was insufficient money around, chapping door-to-door would do the job. Maree wasn't allowed to cut corners. Each bird had to look pristine, or else the problems would begin again.

Sixteen years ago, there had been a landslip, a result of fracking in the mountains, or else the will of the gods or the heavy rains that winter, depending on who you asked, the townsfolk or the local authority. The primary school had been buried. The graveyard, the local supermarket. Parents out getting the shopping were killed at the same instant as their children. Little ones were fretting over their times tables or running the beep test in the gym when the windows on the Northern side of the buildings all caved in against the tonnes of oozing dark brown mud and shale fragments. The tide of mud had reached to the sea, then spilled over into it, like the contents of luggage tipping off the edge of a bed. The sound of the falling earth burst the eardrums of half the survivors.

The weather had grown unusually dry about that time, and so the mud became dust, and blew about the place, sometimes hanging in a cloud so dark that the town seemed to live in the half-light of a partial eclipse. It was just as the last loads of dirt were being ferried into the sea that the bird appeared to Tobey Silks. Silks, a dull man otherwise and new-made widower, saw the bird appear in the sky as he came to open his grocery shop. He said it had glided down from the roof, gentle like. It was the size of a partridge, plump bodied, with this great glorious long tail that fanned out, a bit like a version of a peacock's, but whiter, and coiled at the tips. It stood on the bins near the bread pallets, and it cocked its head at him, and then flipped its feathers out – here Tobey would try to explain exactly how it had flipped them, spreading his finger wide and putting it over his balding head. Like this, he'd say, but beautiful. Then it opened its mouth, and sang.

Tobey was deaf at that time, though he had since regained part of his hearing. But he knew it was singing, and he knew that it was the most wonderful sound in the world. The noise of a rainforest, full of sparks and crackling leaves and twirls of other bird and animal cries, and water bubbling downwards, and animals scouting in the water, and fish gaping and hovering in portions of light. That the birdsong came from the far past, a world without humans and human suffering. All this was a lot, coming from Tobey Silks.

It was he who bought the first stuffed Superb Lyrebird, and put it in the grocery window, so that everyone could see what he meant.

A year later, the second landslip hit the town on the same day and hour, and the third was exactly one year from that, and the fourth. Silk's Convenience was left untouched. From then on, the deaf outnumbered the hearing, and local organisers set up sign language classes alongside the bereavement counselling sessions in the meeting hall. Nobody knew the sign for Superb Lyrebird, so they used the one Tobey Silks had come up with. It happened that each person who had lost a loved one came to see the bird. As if visited by a spirit, something alien and perfect, though it rarely did anything but scratch about, and sing, in a way that sent rainforests into the mind, holding back the smell of mud and crushed concrete with brilliant greens and cool clear water. Soon everyone afflicted had a stuffed lyrebird. Maree thought it a little unlikely herself. She couldn't say much about the loss of the town, since she had only been a little girl when the fourth landslide had happened, home ill from school, in safety. She barely remembered her brothers, let along her classmates, and she had never had a vision of any bird. Still, she took them up on the anniversary of each slip to the old armoury on the hill, and arranged them to watch over all, from early morning to sunset. If nothing happened, that, just that, was the miracle.

When the last of the lyrebirds had been set in elegant order on the wall, Maree signed to a window below, hoping her mother had got up and was pointing the telescope her way. The sign for vigil light. Up, across the valley, ran a ripple of gentle wind, that reached the silvering filamentaries of the birds and ruffled them a little, though not, as Maree remembered, holding her own hair, the way the real birds did, in the videos she had been shown.

Flour: Prolog

Hamish Scott

Athin a flour is aa we need tae ken
the mortal an immortal life o men

Fare

Christie Williamson

Now that all of the ways have been found
and all of the paths have been followed round
what's left to wither into the ground?
What shoots for the easter sun?

Here where the wind from the Firth of Clyde
blows snide in the face of human worth
who can ignore the music of hope?
Who can search the shore for more
than the crush of concrete tides?

This is the body of life
broken for time to reclaim.

This is the blood of a dying god
shed that the skin may grow whole again.

Winterhill

Catherine Graham

The heat glossing their backs.
Moon licking the river
white. They thrive

at night. Born nocturnal,
they smell the rub
of dew slipping out.

To see through darkness
blocked by moon, cloud, star.
Where is the water? The bullfrog knows.

The spring peeper. Their growing chorus
itches the air. There is no gate
to pass. Just a metallic

scent they cannot detect—
what hits, kills. Curled
into carcass, rot, on beds

of gravel and dirt, they lie
ready to receive a birth
of fly and maggot. But the lifting

fog is a trail becoming
from the non-soul's
heat, the organs' stop.

All instinct from inside
them now furring air
with whitish vale, shadow's

trick of weight. Here is where
the dead live on – ghost
animals – in a world

called Winterhill. They've
become a floating pond,
a threshold of in-between,

moist portal where water
finds water and fixes
to air—

        there, there.

Leash of Deer

Catherine Graham

Untamable creatures,
pelt-spotted as trout lily,
camouflaged umber, tawny

branched with satellite ears,
air-cupped to the heart-
beat of the ground.

Extended line between
sun-dawn moon-dusk—
a leash of deer, that

teasing word: *leash*.
Which site brought forth
the first? Allowed

leggy form lift?
Up and off the forest
floor into white-tailed

leaps or red or roe.
No matter. Kill. Suffocation.
Quick throat slit.

Kill and stop the leash
of deer from spreading out
so when that fall night

rears, a father driving
home, one road
away from home,

no cloven-hoofed ungulate
on Stonemill Road,
parting from a field

of parting corn,
from stalk and husk
and rustle beside

a frog-thick croaking
ditch to trigger
panic – the swerve – a father

would have made it back
to bed, exhaling O's
of alcohol through greying

shades of stubble and a daughter
would awaken to the muffle
of his morning snores

through cedar walls and not
the 3 am knocking at her
bedroom door, the waiting cop.

Old Mattress

Ian Burgham

Old mattress partially
lying under the corrugated
steel roofing sheet behind the railway fence –
the stains a reminder of her groaning –

grandma's death –
the bowels emptying take a bit of time
after the last breath-rattle
when eyes are fingered closed.

Then the shit on the sheets –
straight into the washing machine.
The smell of the room takes much longer to erase
though you haven't visited the house for years.

She suffered need, a hunger
faith could not satisfy.
No God could meet
a desire so great.

You too have fought this fight.
Grapes are seedless, full of seeds.
It's a switch... a brain switch
for which the heart has the password
you can't keep straight –

you search for it as though on-line –
give the code to prove who you are,
the name of the first street you grew up on,
the name of your best friend when you were five,
your first dog. The place where you first heard
your parents were divorcing. The hour
when your brother died.

Sometimes, when you're full
of danger, you remember –
angels or other servants of God
send the memory to you. Till then
you shudder in the dark
leaning on the windowsill
in grandma's bedroom.

Séance, A Poetics

Jeanette Lynes

        The bride's throat began to hollow,
to fenestrate.
Gone spindrift, like all brides. I know
how this sounds but *please* this once
suspend your disbelief.
We'd inhaled our share of exploding flash powder.
The man in charge measured levels.
His new anastigmatic lens
rattled silver, wires went herky.
The deal table stormed, pitched us
forward in our chairs like we rode rickety tractors.
Our Medium, a small
Scottish woman, scoured houses all day,
still held a soap-curd scent.
Our medium, pure metaphor: a pudding having a seizure.

Imagine a semi-colon here, quick, a voice said; and I did.
A parlor with grammar wields a tight ship.
Conditions must be airtight and not blathering.
On burled walnut shelves Kodak's latest, lit red,
roosted hawkish. The best doily quaked.
A tall cabinet mimed antique telephone kiosk.
And outside, the stock market's awful disquiet,
its sunken, hermetic sentence run on.

And on. You didn't suppose this ended well,
did you? I blinked back a mist of
missing my mother. Held hands within the circle
(to my left, the respected barrister's palm
sweaty; he wanted *his* mother, too).
Whatever it took to scrape through.

The medium huffed: 'you missed a spot'
(dust diviner). Her throat sparked a hymn-tremolo.

Somewhere a bride lofted beyond questions.
In her own spangled dust.
A broach frothed before us. Meringue. No – *a face*
we chimed and no dissent, noted the note-taker. *A face.*

Shrunk within the small fogs
of ourselves we each saw the face we saw.
My mother, hungry, young –
I longed to retro-wire her the money
for high school. Longed with such intent
I bit my mouth-lining red, missed a spot.
Bit better, harder
for full blood.

Even when the bride lost her throat,
ripped open by a wolverine wearing a pillbox
we believed in a township beyond the cabinet,
pastoral, with church picnics
where smitten dead boys bid for pies
baked by pretty dead girls.
Failing all else pastry
provides a reason to be here at all.
Pastry. And hope. Stupid, stupid hope
and its conjunctions and

Mother I'm still here
in the vapor years still
making things up, hoping
something will come of it;
still stuttering through the brume
For that's what a poem does. Doesn't it.

The Last Sturgeon

Steven Heighton

Deltawave shadows
of his deeds
and didn'ts, slid
under his shoes
like fillet knives, severing
soles from soil,
so he always walked
a little above his life,
not knowing it was
his life, while it waned
from waking-coma
to coma.
          Came a land-
locked night
he dreamed that he'd
landed the last sturgeon in the world
and she looked bad—
shrunken, bludgeoned,
a blue-ribbed CAT-scan
of herself, her buckled
gills gawping,
a foam of green roe
welling from her mouth.
Each egg
was a tear, a tiny, entreating
vowel he couldn't quite hear
as he cast round the boat (now morphing
into a mountain shack)
for *water*, the merest
rainpool, he panicked,
or glacial stream,

my dearest,
my loved one,
let me bear you back
to haven—by river
the ocean
is never far.

Wakey wakey

Christie Williamson

Rise an wipe da brine
fae anunder dy green een
an keep hit clean as du picks

dy wye up trow da fug,
da rain an da gravity
o da forces arrayed agin de.

If du canna dø da time,
dis pliss'll surely dø as fine
as ony iddir, or if du feels

laek brakkin trow da clood
du'll dø weel ta pack a punch
abön dy graet ideas. Du'll be fine

bi da time du's stopped da rot,
clocked da blunt force trauma,
med da obstacles du hed fur brakkfist
be gone.

How a·Poet Must

Steven Heighton

How a poet, impossible, must be
is – unenclosed wholly and yet

clamped shut – pores open
like portholes to the world

in welcome, yet unbreachable
as a safe, or carapace, case-

hardened against carious
words, spurious charms,

the germs of indigestible
trivia, by the gigabyte:

trite contagion. (Yet be curious
to the killing point.)

How must the poet flow?
Between these poles, impossibly,

and his goal, her goal – instantiate
in a phrase or stanza one moment

of flayed presence, in ways
no I-mind could counterfeit.

Testament
(after Killochries by Jim Carruth)

Christie Williamson

Afore da wird, did da sharp solstice sun
burn da een ony less i da thrice iced
thrill o da bare Jül hill?

Wioot da book ta bind da willin
an da wance wanted fur mair
as da pooir o dir shoodirs, wha'd heed

da swalloo's promees o a lang nicht's wark?
Wha'd rise wi da sang o redemptive draems
still sweet i dir lugs ta pit brakkfist

on da table? Wha'd wakk da verges
o plooed an falloo fields? Wha'd fin
an mend da hols i da fence

whaar da wild wirld oot ower
could win in, whaar da saddled service
o a free man's haert could brakk oot?

The Gutter Interview:

Angela Catlin

The Gutter Interview: Angela Catlin

Anglea Catlin is a photographer and photo-journalist based in Glasgow. She has been described as one of the most gifted and experienced photographers in the world and has won numerous awards for her photography including Feature Photographer of the Year at the UK National Picture Editor Awards and Scottish Photographer of the Year on two occasions.

Angela has worked in places such as Rwanda, Gaza, Guatemala, Haiti and Columbia. Working with Journalist Billy Briggs she has won Amnesty International's Scottish Media Award and was the British winner of the European Union Journalist Award in 2007. Her focus is often on human rights and global injustice, but she is known also for two books of portraits made thirty years apart, *Natural Light* (1985) and *Natural Light II* (2016), which bring together pictures of Scotland's best known writers.

G: Can you tell us a bit about how you became a photographer, and where this project, *Natural Light*, came from?

A: Wow, gee whizz. Well, I worked as a painter and decorator for Craigmillar Festival Society. There were two teams, a NIT team – Neighbourhood Improvement Team – and a CAT team – Community Arts Team – and I remember mum was working in the information office at the Craigmillar Festival Society and she did not want me to apply for a job there. She just wanted me getting a proper job. I had tried for the police, I was a police cadet for six months, I didn't like the strait-jacket of the uniform, as soon as you walked outside, you were on call. I was just a cadet and people would take the piss, ask me stupid questions, stuff like that. It was just embarrassing, and at the point there was no trousers, just a skirt, and I felt a bit vulnerable, wearing this uniform. And it was Craigmillar don't forget, Greendykes. So anyway, I lasted about six months. Couple of dead bodies too many. Which in retrospect I shouldn't probably have been at the scene of. Funnily enough I went back with these stories to my brother, who then made a career in the police. I used to tell him what was going on at the end of the day and he got more and more interested. Well, I chucked it, and he joined.

So, I was part of this neighbourhood improvement scheme, as a painter and decorator, did that for about a year and had a wacko time. Just doing up old folks homes, and folk who couldn't afford it, there was a gaffer, two guys and me, and I just really enjoyed doing it. Then after a year a job came up as a photographer's assistant, and someone said to me, 'you apply for that photographers job' and I was like that, *I've never taken a photograph really, all I've got's my Instamatic that I got for my 15th birthday.* And they said 'it's ok, you don't need to have had any experience.' But I'm not even visual you know. But I went for the interview and had to sneak in and out past mum. Afterwards, councillor Davie Brown said to my mum 'tell Angie she got the job.' And she went 'What job! What's she doing.' So that was me, I was on the

CAT team, Community Arts Team, and I was assistant photographer to John Brown. He taught me everything, much better than any photography course could or would. He was just so generous with his teaching. But I couldn't get the light thing at all. He'd say to me 'that light's so wonderful' and 'that light's just perfect,' and I wasn't getting it at all, I couldn't see what he was talking about. And then – this was five months in – I was going in on the bus, just near Duddingston Loch and the sun was just coming up, and there was this early morning light, and I saw it, and that was it. I saw it, I saw the light, and that was me for the next thirty years. I think that's what established my love of looking at light, working with natural light, light that's god given, rather than artificial.

G: So did you then see it as a way for you to become a journalist, or did you want to be an artist, or a commercial photographer?

A: At that point I wanted to do portraits of everybody. Scottish Writers, Scottish everybody, whatever. So I approached the Arts Council with the idea of a book of portraits, but they said it was too wide a spectrum, just choose one focus. And they didn't know my work or what I could do, you know I didn't have any work. So, I got six portraits together and then they gave me the grant. And I was over the moon. And I got to travel the length and breadth of the UK, just doing portraits, I did all in 2¼ format and it was all natural light.

G: So Natural Light was your first piece of work then.

A: Yeah, but after I finished that I didn't see myself going down the portrait line, there just wasn't that kind of work available. And I really wanted to work in newspapers. I'd just been doing little jobs. I remember a shift in a Chinese restaurant by the Grosvenor, on Ashton Lane, and I had talked them into giving me a trial at lunch time, they give me a big basin of prawns to shell and I failed miserably, so they gave me a free lunch and told me that I wasn't a very good Chinese cook. I walked out of there and there were two phone boxes just on the Byres Rd and I went into one and phoned the picture desk of The Glasgow Herald. It was the assistant editor and I was really so nervous, but I thought I am just gonna try it, and they said 'yeah ok, he's not here today, come in tomorrow and we'll have a chat.' So, I went in and I had Natural Light by then, and at first they were giving me arts and portrait work, not really journalism stories. There was one weekend and I had done a picture of this artist, Stephen Campbell, and I hadn't heard and I hadn't heard, and I thought ach the picture must have been rubbish, I'll never get used again. And I was waiting for my brother on the Saturday morning in a roll shop on Royal Exchange Square and there were papers, so I opened The Herald. Back then the arts pull out was broadsheet size, full page, and my portrait was the full length of the paper. I was over the moon. So Monday morning I went up and asked is there any more work? I thought you know, it was worth a try. Unfortunately, (for Stuart, not me) one of the staff photographers, had had a heart attack. It was a sort of being in the right place at the right time. So they said, go down to the local community farm they've got this new animal in the petting farm or something similar. They'd give me these little jobs. And that was my apprenticeship really. The more they saw I was capable of, the more they gave me, and I just sneaked up the scale of the job. So that when I was introduced to news stories I was ready, and I ended up getting away from the portraits to photojournalism, and I went from freelance to staff at *The Herald*.

G: And was that where you wanted to be then? Was the book a stepping stone to the photo journalism?

A: No. I didn't have a clue what I was gonna do. I just had this thing that I didn't know what the opportunities were. Now I would, but then I just had this idea of getting my pictures into the papers, doing that. I had a good few years, won Scottish photographer of the year twice. At that stage I think I was the only female news photographer apart from Leslie in Fife. I felt a bit claustrophobic in the newspapers though, even though I was enjoying it. And in my own time I was doing work for the magazine, *The Herald Magazine*, which could have sold on the shelves by itself I always thought, it was great. Great picture editor, great editor. And so I just started generating stories for them, and I would find a like-minded journalist who was interested in doing the words. And we'd go off and do whatever it was and that's how I actually ended up working with Billy Briggs. We both left *The Herald* at the same time and we were both interested in human rights and social issues, and we'd been doing those kind of jobs together and we kept on doing that. But then, there was a bit of a hiatus for me later. We'll not bother about it in this interview. But, when I came back from the Tsunami, I was very ill for a while. After that I didn't think I'd be taking pictures ever again to tell you the truth. I

just, I had total fatigue. However it left me, I just felt drained: couldn't hardly move one foot in front of the other, sleeping twenty four hours. But one way or another, I got back on track. Maybe nine months down the line. And I was lucky, cos I had support from *The Herald Magazine*, they would give me small jobs. At first I'd ask 'is there gonna be anyone else there' I was totally terrified; it was like rebuilding yourself all over again, from ground zero. Anyway, I wouldn't be able to do that in any other circumstance. Just with the help of friends I got myself back together again. And then, I was back. But I guess I wasn't quite back. I remember me and Billy going to Guatemala to do a story about violence against women, femicide. And I was absolutely drained; when we weren't working I was sleeping. So, it was slow but I was on the road.

G: Off to Gaza?

A: That's right yeah, it was already under siege. There was nothing going in or out, people weren't going in or out. Medical supplies weren't going in. It was a daily struggle for the Gazan people. So basically we were going out to cover the story and the difficulties they were facing. And we met some amazing people. There's a million and a half Gazans living in a prison, it's just like they are being squeezed dry, physically, mentally, emotionally, everything. We met fishermen who had lost limbs for fishing just outside the designated waters, cos the Israelis had restricted where they could work, which was hardly any area at all. And if they dared to go out of that area the Israeli gunboats would just open fire. The water was pretty polluted near Gaza, and it was forcing the fisherman to go out further, but then they were running the gauntlet of gunfire. And the medical issues as well, kids getting treated for survivable complaints, but never surviving because they weren't getting access to the care they needed. This has always been quite close to me actually, man's inhumanity to man. What they've been through, the West Bank as well. It's all going on under the radar right now. It's all still happening on a daily basis, but other things have overtaken it. I saw a story the other day, from the West Bank, where they are knocking down the houses of Palestinian families, that have been there for centuries, and the Bedouin as well, and if they don't knock down their homes themselves, they would have to pay money to the Israelis to knock them down. It's just the worst treatment; beyond belief to me. I'd like to get back out there actually, cover that story more.

G: What do you think your photos are doing in these two contexts, the portraits and the journalism?

A: It's telling a story about the person. I think that's it. The first book, the first *Natural Light* was much tighter, the portraits were tighter, you know. This time I wanted them to breathe, I think having been in journalism and looking at the wider picture, and seeing more of a story, it informed things. So this time I wanted to create a bit more environment around them, let the subject breathe a bit. There's some I have gone in more *map of the face*, but not so many. More are urban landscape/environmental portrait.

G: And do you think you have to give something of yourself to it? Are you telling the story, directing the narrative, or is the story there, be it James Robertson or Gaza,

and you're just uncovering it.

A: No, I'm not directing it. Ok, I've got my views, but I still have to be objective, and tell both sides. It's balanced, but it just happens, you can't not see what's going on, so often you can see whether somebody is lying: whether the story is true or not.

G: So you're an observer?

A: When I'm doing human rights reportage, yeah, I'm more of an observer. But doing the portraits it's more directing. And the backdrop was as important I think as the person I was photographing. I like to turn up about half an hour to forty minutes before and have a good scope around and see what would make for a good backdrop. Sometimes I didn't get the chance – like with Alasdair Gray – I think I was in and out in fifteen minutes [laughs] but at other times I would just stay as long as it was needed. It worked anyway: whether I stayed fifteen minutes or I stayed a couple of hours, I had what I wanted when I left.

G: Is there any portrait in the books that you think the context – the landscape – of it is particularly important to you?

A: I think Douglas Dunn [in a rolling field of stubble and round straw bales]. I felt that reflected his work. And we were chasing the light that day – the sun was going down and because we'd spent time chatting we had to jump in my car, and race against the dying of the winter's light. I worked during winter light, from October to March, so the light was going down at about half-three or four and not only were we still looking for my backdrop but we had to get it before the sun totally disappeared and changed the whole picture. So as soon as I saw it I just ran the car into the field, and Douglas ran over to the bales, we didn't have long to do it, but as soon as I saw it that was just so lucky, so lucky. The light was just perfect and it worked. And there are pictures like Alan Bissett's. His picture is at Grangemouth, where he grew up, in its shadow, so there is a bit of that story in the picture. And Ronald Frame's a big Italian film fan – Fellini and so on – so underneath the M8 suited that urban landscape feel of his Glasgow. And Alasdair was just needs must. When I got in touch with him – I was so pleased he said yes and agreed to it – and he said 'But I remember thirty years ago you didn't spend very long taking the picture, could you do that again?' And I said yes, no problem, and then when I turned up he'd forgotten I was going to be turning up at all, he wasn't in, and I'd gone off again, but fortunately I was still in the West End [of Glasgow], down in Fopp, when I got a call back. Alasdair was home so I went back up the road and he was working away at the window. I'd just got my jacket off and Morag made me a cup of tea, Alasdair had moved over to his desk and it was just lovely, the light at the window, he had illustrations that he was working on for a book, so I just said if you could just carry on with your work Alasdair, forget I'm here – not knowing that he *would* forget that I was there – and so I started doing some pictures of him just working away. And then I said ok, just glance up now, and he just said 'You're really distracting me here!' [laughs] So I said it won't take long, you know, so I took a couple of pictures where he sat, and the one that is on the cover [of Natural Light II] I went in closer, whereas the other one that is used inside the book is more of a journalistic photograph, telling the story.

But I must have been in and out in fifteen minutes – I had a promise to keep!

G: How was it photographing people thirty years apart? Did they feel like the same people? Jim Kelman for instance, had you seen him in the intervening years?

A: No, it's amazing! That was the thing; it just felt that when you chapped the door and they opened it and it could've been last week! I mean, visually people have changed so much in that time, but it just felt very comfortable. I never felt uneasy at all. It was as if that thirty years had just melted away. It was quite amazing – as if there had been contact in the intervening years. Stewart Conn, Liz [Lochhead], Jim [Kelman]. Jim's got grumpier in his old age (sorry about that, Jim). So I found that bit fascinating. I think there are maybe ten of the people from the original book in this one.

Quite often, if the writer decided where they'd like the picture to be taken I'd be led by them. I'd just let it go where it flowed and was also led by the writers . My very first writer was Christopher Brookmyre, and I had an idea that I'd photograph him at Love Street, as he's a big St Mirren supporter. So he said, 'Yeah, ok, that's fine.' But then he says, 'But also I go walking down by Bothwell Castle trying to untangle lines and where I'm going, stuff like that.' So I suggested what about if we do both then, one of you outside the stadium with your St Mirren scarf, and then we'll go down to Bothwell Castle and he was dead right. He was dead right – that was the picture. Kirsty Logan wanted to go down to the beach at Culzean Castle which is lovely, because that meant something personal to her. I think mostly people were in their own environment, either at home or close to, but I would just be led by them. If they didn't feel strongly about where they wanted their picture taken that was fine as well, but it was a very flexible situation – I just let it go where it wanted. And whatever the light was on the day, that's what it was as well, so there was no failure as such; it was whatever it was, wherever it went, whatever the circumstance, whatever the light was there. And there wasn't one where I thought I wish I'd done it this way, or that the light was rubbish – it all worked out. In fact I was really lucky, that winter was one of the driest we've ever had, so I think it was only a couple where it was actually raining out of, what, 56 people? It was quite incredible. And that light again! I was photographing late morning or early afternoon, and it was just really good. I mean I couldn't have done it this winter – it was just so wet! [chuckles] Well, of course i could have, but it was easier with no rain, and that light.

G: Did you worry about people not liking their portraits, or does that not matter too much to you?

A: Hmmm. I wanted the people to like them ok, because they'll have to look at it for quite a long time! [laughs] But I just shot it the way how I instinctively felt. There was no kind of 'well they would look better this side or–' I just didn't think about that. And I think that works for it. If you are comfortable with the person that reflects as well, and there wasn't anybody that I didn't get on with. I think I've got used to dipping in and out of people's lives. It's the same in photojournalism. Going off and doing a story, you are in people's lives for short but quite vivid time. I don't know how to describe that really. I mean, I always feel this

when we're working away, I think, god we go into these people's lives just for that short time, and we can leave it, we go back, but they are still there, and that... sometimes it grates a bit, you know? Of course I'm trying to tell a story, I'm trying to raise awareness about whatever situation, but I don't want to feel like I've used people at all. In fact, it was good when I did the Life after Iraq project – that was a refugee story. Most of the refugees had gone to Syria so Billy and I went to Damascus where thousands of the Iraqi refugees had gone – though now of course they will have had to have moved again – and we were comparing the situation, Syria at that point had taken about a million Iraqi refugees, and Glasgow had quite a few coming in at that point as well, so the Scottish Refugee Council commissioned Billy and I to go to Syria and do a story on the hardships and the daily life of being a refugee and what they were facing over there, and looking at what the parallels were with Glasgow. I'm still friendly with a family from that – that's about eight years now and I was over seeing them the other day. They're off and running now, you know, but I was involved in their lives for a long time. Because Hanna arrived just with the three kids, she was on her own, at that point – her husband wasn't over yet – and so now I just feel like part of their family. I can just turn up and they are just so welcoming, and I really care about them. The mum was so protective about the kids. They lived in the Red Road flats, and she wouldn't let them out of her sight. So I'd say that I'd take them – though I had to build up a trust as well, you know? So we'd just go and play football down at the pitches at Red Road, or take them swimming (the mum coming along) and then she kind of said ok – and Omar, who is 19 now, was really keen on football – so I got him into a wee team and then I started taking him to training or to the games, and the mobile would go maybe ten times during the game; *it's ok Hanna, I can still see him and he's fine, he's playing football and don't worry he'll be home soon.* And then we'd be in the car and she'd be phoning, but that was just the legacy of the trauma that they'd experienced, especially Hanna, and what had happened over in Baghdad. That's been satisfying and rewarding, so I feel I kind of readdress it a wee bit. I mean, I can't do anything on a daily basis for the people in Gaza – I can't adopt everybody, but I can do something here, and I've got another family that I met through the Freedom From Torture organisation [based down near the Gorbals] Billy and I were doing a feature about them, an exhibition, and I got quite close to Rana and Tehmina and the kids as well, so I'm really lucky – I've got two surrogate families. And I get well fed [laughs] it's the only time I eat properly, when I'm over visiting one of them! And that's fine. I feel happy about that, because I've given back a wee bit, I'm not just going into people's lives and coming away again.

G: But is the act of going into people's lives not helping?

A: I don't really feel... I mean, they feel they are left behind or something. 'What did I gain from that? I give these people' – me or Billy or whoever – 'I let them into my life and gave them my story.' And we just take it away. What's left? That's what I feel. And that's why having Hanna and Rana, families that I can give back a wee bit. So Hanna's family, they're fine. They're adults mostly –

Omar doesn't need me to do the football run unfortunately [laughs] he can do it himself; I taught him to drive, so they're all fine. And Ahmed the husband is over now as well. And another wee unexpected arrival. When I was over in Rome, at the British School, I came back and the kids were saying, 'Do you notice anything different.' and I was saying no she looks fine, putting on a bit of weight or something, and the kids were giggling and laughing, and it turns out she was pregnant. Adam is four now.

The British School was a big change. I think I was happily going along in my little photojournalism life, and when the British School came out of nowhere with this three month fellowship in Rome. That was just an eye-opener. It was fantastic, just mixing, you know, being with artists and the buzz that was created around the place; a twenty-four hour library, original Piranesis, a Caravaggio in every church(just about) and the culture of Rome – the life of the streets. I love life on the street, and at first my idea had been that I might do a people trafficking story, in Rome: girls coming from Nigeria into Burkina Faso, and then into Europe, Rome is quite a bit of a hub for people trafficking. But it really became apparent quickly that without the language I would just hit bureaucracy and red tape and I thought I can't do this, or the three months are going to go like that [clicks fingers]. So I just thought right, ok, why I started photography was because I really loved Cartier Bresson's street photography. I'm just going to spend my time doing street photography, and that's what I did. And it was during that time that I thought, maybe it is time to revisit *Natural Light*. Creative Scotland were so supportive right from the off, and the late Gavin Wallace was so encouraging. I don't think it would have happened if I didn't have the British School at Rome experience. It was enlightening for me. And I remember saying I think you want somebody younger for this [laughs]. I mean why would they want me to do it – an old hack. But they did and I'm so glad, it was just the best ever, a fantastic experience, and it opened my eyes to the art world as well. It was like university and gap year – which I'd never had – all in one, rolled into three months. It was so intense, really intense. I loved it.

G: And will you do any other art books? Anything else you want to focus on?

A: I'd like to. I'd love to do more portraits, like with *Natural Light II*. I was wondering, is there room for one on Scottish artists? I don't know. And I've got a couple of ideas for reportage stories. I've always been interested in Native Americans and there was an artist called George Catlin – same surname as me – 200 years ago he went round different reservations. In the face of real danger, he visited reservations and documented their way of life and did portraits as well, so I find kind of an affinity with him somehow as well. I'd like to follow in his footsteps. So I've been doing a wee bit of research on him.

G: That might bring together the two things you're talking about, in a way, the sort of human rights reportage and the...

A: Exactly. I don't want to be all doom and gloom – that's Billy and I's name for each other – [laughs]. That's our double act, 'doom and gloom'. I don't want it to be like that, cos we've had all that as well and I just think, let's have a positive look at what's happened to people...I know there's such problems in the reservations but I wanted to have a rounded look and not be too negative. I mean there'll have been thousands of people who have made a success of their lives as well. So, I quite fancy doing that. Again it's reportage and portrait the same as what George Catlin did 200 years ago.

G: It's a tacky question but do you have a favourite book photo where you've taken a photograph that means the most to you?

A: From the book?

G: Yeah either, both, from the book and from your career.

A: Yeah, I've never really thought about it. Oh... China! One in China. Yeah, I had gone out to China. I went out three times, this was my second visit before they were flooding the four hundred mile stretch of the Yangtze when they were building the Three Gorges Dam and I wanted to document life before the waters came and all signs of *the China before* disappeared, and just photograph it, a way of life that's gone. So I was really the only European... I would never bump into anybody else white in the places I was going on these trips up the Yangtze river. I remember waiting one early morning for the boat and I just saw this tableaux in front of me of these different characters and it was amazing! It was like a moving painting and I just raised the camera – I had to keep my camera up for quite a while and then keep the one eye open just watching. The challenge was that I didn't want anybody looking at the camera and it's difficult there because I'm different, they want to look and wonder who I am, why I'm there. So I just stood still. I don't know if there's maybe 8 or 10 people in the picture, there might be one that maybe looks as if they're looking at the camera but that's my picture, I love that. Along with a Chinese miner, those are the only two pictures of mine I've got up on the wall. Just the setting, the people, the characters; it was a portrait of life on the Yangtze, that's what it was. So I'd love to do something like that again and the Native American thing is as close to that as I can think of. There's another dam I think in South America somewhere that's gonna be built and that's gonna cause possibly all sorts of problems for indigenous people losing land again, so I think – how many people were displaced – maybe a million people were displaced along that stretch in China, and the same thing would happen. So I was thinking about having a look at that story as well. I mean, the big environmental impact and the little people that have got no voice as usual.

G: But first you've got *Natural Light II* to launch. What do you think people are looking for in those portraits?

A: To see the person behind the words. A lot of people won't have an idea of what Ali Smith looks like or Alison Kennedy or Denise Mina or Louise Welsh, so I think they're interested, it's just curiosity. Seeing the person behind the words just adds another dimension doesn't it, to what they're reading. That's what fascinates me as well cos I'm not very good at using words, I'm not, y'know, word friendly. I love reading but I'm not very good at using them and I think maybe that's why I was drawn to photographing writers. Trying to understand a wee bit more how they use these words.

G: But you're a storyteller as well. Not just as a photographer.

A: Me?

G: Yeah.

A: Yeah. Yeah. I like that. Telling a story. [long pause] I'm just thinking, that would make a nice portrait view [laughs, gestures]. Just where you are there and the kind of luminous lights off to one side and just…that's excellent. Shame there's no a photographer in the room!

But yeah I'm just kinda… words faze me. All the words, they've been used. It's like stepping on a crack in the pavement, y'know, when you were a kid and you were trying to avoid stepping on the cracks. It's like how do you avoid using the same word? How do you change words into a different story? The same words! It absolutely fascinates me. I know it's so simple and straightforward and obvious but how can they use all these same words and come out with totally different stories? I wanted to see these people that can do that.

G: And was there any one of them that was an absolute fucking nightmare to photograph?

A: Alasdair! [raucous laughter]. No, he wasn't really, just carnaptious! He just wanted to get on with his work [laughs]. I think he thought I'd just kinda snuck in off the street and appeared in front of him!

G: I would've thought one of the grand old men, MacKay Brown or McCaig or someone might have been difficult.

A: No. I was kind of in awe of them – as with Alasdair, still, thirty years later – y'know? Just being in their presence and Sorely McLean, as you said, George MacKay Brown, Ian Crichton Smith, Edwin Morgan, Norman McCaig, they were just all, just really good guys.

G: I think I said before the McKay Brown picture is my absolute favourite just because he's this wild Orcadian figure in this little hallway in this very suburban looking setting.

A: I know, well the thing is that's right, because I went all the way to Orkney and I photographed him in a porch. Well I was nervous as you say, but I can't get over that. What was I thinking about? Why wasn't he kind of striding out across the beaches or the dunes or whatever in Orkney with a landscape backdrop! But for some reason, known not even to me, I did the picture there. And again Sorely McLean, I photographed him on Raasay. Why is he not out in the landscape? And I have no idea, I've no idea, but now with my experience for thirty years in between in newspapers and doing photo-journalism and telling stories, I think, made these portraits very different from the first.

G: I think they are different but I think that McLean or McKay Brown in a domestic setting tells a story too though. Because in a way you romanticise these particularly 'island' poets with these big outdoor things, when really if you live on an island most of your time is spent in a hallway or in a kitchen, you know, they're not striding across dunes composing, their grafting, trying to write in their wee rooms.

A: Good point. Good point. Yeah! See you can use words better than me, but that's right. I remember when I was photographing Jim Kelman. In fact when he saw his poem beside, I say it's a poem, his observation beside his portrait in the first book was 'same t-shirt, might've known'. And he had me convinced when I was doing his portrait thirty years later than that was his same t-shirt on the heater [laughs]. Honestly, I was nearly convinced. I asked Jim, can we do the photograph along by the canal, in Maryhill up in the area where he stays and he said, 'Aww naw', he wisnae having any of that, 'we'll just do it up in the study'. I think it was the same clock on the walls as the first picture thirty years before, y'know. So just being very open minded or whatever turns up, whatever happens in front of me, that's what I love. I just love photographing or interpreting what's happening. To be invisible, that's a photographer's greatest gift. To become invisible. That's what I try to do when I'm doing photojournalism. But it always... I think there's this kind of dropping in and out of people's lives is what I do best. I was thinking about that the other day. I don't hang about. I just... I just want a taste of people's lives, I don't want to live them [laughs].

Ronnie wisnae the bonniest mind an wi a few cans in mi his frizzy white hair made him look like he had been electrocuted, an his eyes were aw dark as tar wi sharp flecks glintin in them like shards of smashed glass. Ah mind the room felt aw spinny (ah couldnae handle ma drink back then) an ah felt sick.

Oot Ma Heid
Rhona Miller

Oot ma Heid

Rhona Miller

Ah had tae leave them ah'd nae choice. Ah'll say that now an ah sade it then. He left me wi four weans an a jist wanted somethin fir myself. His Ma took in the eldest two fir me till ah got back on ma feet. An ma neighbour Marie said she'd watch over the little wans till ah went oot fir a bit—*ah needed to get oot.* A mind ah started walkin as fast as ah could, ah didnae really know where ah was headed, ah jist wanted away frae the hoose, away frae the weans an away frae Union Road. Ah walked doon past the Miners club in ah wis aboot tae walk up the road that takes yi past the fields an up tae the Meddies when it started chuckin it doon. Great big dollops ay rain that soaked right through mi, so ah thought better of it an ah headed back towards the shop, ah thought mibbe some chocolate an a pack a fags would sort me oot. A wis comin oot a Costcutters when ah bumped into Ronnie puffin on a dowt outside the bookies next door. Me in Ronnie used tae have a wee snog in that afore ah met the weans Da, everyone sade he wis an alky but he seemed fine tae me that day.

We stood an chatted aboot the auld days an it wisnae long afore we were back inside his wan bed wi a couple a cans a cold Super lager. It felt gid hearing the hiss of that first can as ah cranked open the ringpull an smelled that sweet smell, kindae like those gobstoppers ah used to get when ah wis young. It left a sour bitter taste in ma mouth an ma stomach heaved frae drinking it, bit a didnae say nothing tae Ronnie. Ah wanted, ah *needed,* tae get drunk. Ah felt like ah did when ah wis a bairn, an we had a laugh dancin aboot like eejits tae auld tunes like *Ride oan Time. Such a gid sensation,* ah still love that yin even tho am tae auld tae be dain any dancin these days. A mind thinkin surely am allowed tae have some fun tae, it canny jist be *him* leavin me wi all the stress of bringin up the weans on ma ain.

Ronnie wisnae the bonniest mind an wi a few cans in mi his frizzy white hair made him look like he had been electrocuted, an his eyes were aw dark as tar wi sharp flecks glintin in them like shards of smashed glass. Ah mind the room felt aw spinny (ah couldnae handle ma drink back then) an ah felt sick. Ronnie said fir mi to lie doon on his bed, which wis jist a mattress on the flair nae bedcovers or nothin, an then he started pullin at the waist band of ma jeans, tryin tae get ma zip doon. He right struggled tryin to get them aff, they were still a bit sodden frae the rain, an a wis a bigger lassie back then. Wance he finally got them aff ah mind noticing that ma legs had turned a funny blue colour frae the denim die, an then ah mind jist shuttin ma eyes an let him get oan wi it. He started makin aw these squeallin noises ah'd never heard frae a bloke afore, an his hips were aw bony bumpin intae mi like he wis a skeleton. His skin looked like the colour ay the moon in that dark room wi yi knowthose dirty lookin pot holes oan it, ah mind thinkin wis it dirt or wis it bruises? Any road, ah felt right manky afterwards an when ah sat up ah spewed ma guts up all over masel and the mattress. He wis awright aboot it, didnae seem tae care, bit ah didnae want ma weans tae see me looking like that. So ah called Marie an she said, 'wit time dae yi call this, yer weans have been greetin fir yi aw night,' then she sighed an sade, 'aye they could stay overnight'. But afore ah knew it wan night had rolled intae the next, an ah jist couldnae go back. Back tae the mess, back tae the nappies, back tae the *cryin*. Ah mean Ronnie's place wis a right cowp, bit it didnae seem tae bother me cos we were ay oot.

Next thing ah knew the social were chappin on Ronnie's door sayin ah'd left ma ain weans, that they were in *soiled* claes, an eating mouldy breid. Ah mind ah looked past the social wumen aw dressed in beige an ah spotted Marie, the cow, standin across the road wi some ay her cronnies, her fat orange airms aw folded, lookin like she wis in wan ay them sumo suits.

'Ah telt yi ah wis takin them back to yours Janice,' she shouted, shakin her mangy heid at mi. 'Ah let them stay wi mi fir three nights, cos that's the kinda wumen ah am,' she sade pointin her finger. 'An you sade, aye thanks Marie I'll be headin back later, jist leave them there wi the TV oan, but you never went back did yi? Call yersel a mother?'

'Fuck off an gaun look after yer ain weans,' ah shouted back, the cheek ay her.

*

Then ah said to the snooty lookin social wumen, who did she think she wis lookin doon her bony nose at me, ah telt her tae contact the weans Da he's the wan who ran oaf wi some bint frae doon south. He's nae bothered wi them noo so why the hell should ah?

An ah shut the door.

Ah look now in it's still the same door shut. I've still a drink in ma hand—*shakin*, an ah think, ah *try tae think,* they were better aff withoot me. That hame they went tae had a good name. Ah mind the day they came tae tell mi, a few years later, that ah'd lost ma parental rights, but ah could go tae court if ah wanted tae dispute it, you know, fight fir the weans. Bit ah'd had Kerry-Ann by then an Ronnie, well, he wis quite fond ah throwin his scrawny little fists around, ah felt ah couldnae dae anythin right by him, so ah didnae want tae bring them back tae that. Ah mind ah saw pictures of them wance. The nuns frae the hame sent them an they looked right smart in their school uniforms, an so big ah hardly recognised them. Ah know they went doon south tae stay wi their Da after they left the hame as ah mind ah wis in the Miners wan night an old Jamesy, who knows everythin that's goin oan round here told me breathin his stale whisky breath all over mi. Ah mind thinkin, aye they're alright then an it's aboot time their Da got involved.

Ah don't know if it wis the drink, but ah think ah saw ma youngest William wan day no so long ago. Ah had tae hang ontae ma railins in the garden when ah saw him, ah thought it wis ma ex, it gie me the shivers. He looked right at mi when he walked past an then looked away quick like he wis embarrassed or somat. Ah knew by his eyes no tae even try tae speak wi him, they looked aw black like they'd seen somethin evil. When ah think aboot it he must be aboot thirty noo, but ah can still see him as bein five. Ah mind back when the social wumen brought him round to Ronnie's, carrying him in her airms as if he wis a wee babbay, an she shouted at me; *look at him.* She wis right putting oan the waterworks sayin he wis underweight in neglected an she'd fund him eatin deid flies aff the windae sill. Ah grabbed the socks aff my ain feet an put them oan his, turnin them oer and oer so that his wee feet were aw nice an cosy. Then she took him away. Ah watched her walk doon the path an then ah saw the bigger yins were in her red motor, their faces aw pressed up at the glass, bangin the windae's an greetin in stuff. An ah had tae shut the door. It wis aw ah could dae. Ah tried my best, an sometimes ah think ah shouldnae have had weans but another swig of my can soon melts that thought right oot ma heid.

How Chloe Stern Lost Her Braids

Laura R Becherer

My granny is a Southern Baptist, and she raised me. That should tell you everything you need to know about my life. In case that isn't enough for you, let me give you a few more details: my name is Chloe, I'm sixteen, and I just had a baby.

I'm living with a foster family right now. I miss school, I miss my friends, I miss my dog (Penny). I love my baby, but I wish I'd known more about this whole thing before I got pregnant. I would say I wish I had an abortion, but I don't. I don't want to go to Hell, although I guess it looks like I'm headed there already, anyway. My social worker and I talked about adoption, but I don't see how that's going to help me much. I still have no family, and I can't go back to school anyway. They don't let girls like me back in.

I thought Andrew would marry me; that's what a good Christian girl is supposed to do. That's what my Sunday School teacher always said. But real life isn't like that, I guess. Granny says that good girls don't have sex before they're married, anyway.

I haven't even talked to Andrew in months; his mom and dad won't let me anywhere near him. He probably still loves me. He said he would, forever and ever. He asked me to marry him, and he even gave me a ring. His mom made me give it back, since he took it from her jewelry box. So now it's just me and Mara and Mr. and Mrs. Landers. They only take care of me because of duty. That's what Mr. Landers says during prayers at night. Mrs. Landers says I need a lot of prayers.

Don't think this was Andrew's fault. He's just a boy, and he loved me. I wouldn't have even met him if I'd been in class where I belonged. But I listened to Abby when she said we should skip Religious History and meet Whitney out behind the gym for a cigarette. I don't really smoke, but Whitney was the most popular girl in our school. Her uniform always looked sexy, even though it was the same as ours. If Whitney asked you for a smoke, it meant you were *cool*.

I was standing by my locker after lunch when Abby came up to me and told me that Whitney wanted to meet for a cigarette instead of Religious History, which I don't mind telling you is a pretty boring class. I was brushing my hair, which we're not supposed to do, but my hair was really long and had a tendency to get tangled halfway through the day. Bridgeman's Christian Academy for Young Ladies, that's where I went to school. I was supposed to graduate from there and go to the same Christian college that my dad went to, at least until I got married. Granny says that there's nothing wrong with a light liberal education, that it's becoming. Men don't like boring women, that's what Granny always used to say. My mother was very smart. Granny liked her; she said my mom was ladylike.

But I wasn't thinking of that then. I mean, when Whitney asks you to have a cigarette instead of going to Religious History, the last thing on your mind is going to be is on your mother's virtue or your dad's college. That was my mistake.

I reached behind my heavy Chemistry book to find the pink Victoria's Secret lip gloss Granny doesn't know I have and rubbed some on. Then I brushed my hair a couple more times and fluffed it a little. My hair is the one thing I really used to like about my appearance. Granny never let me get it cut except for trims, so it was *super* long—we're talking blonde braids past my waist. I always left the house with it braided and undid it on the way to school. My last stop of the day was the ladies' room to put it back in order before going home.

Abby and I hid in the ladies' room until the bell rang and we could sneak off. It was a nice day; I like that about Missouri springtime. There was a cool breeze, but it wasn't too windy. Being outside was a lot better than being stuck in Religious History. Religious History is so boring, and Miss Morgan is a sneaky old bat. Sometimes I thought the woman was a mind-reader; she seemed more spy of God than teacher. Meeting Whitney was our main goal, of course, but I tossed my head a little in the free air as we walked the crunchy gravel path that led behind the brick gym. Being outside was just fun.

We headed for the big oak tree that separated the soccer field from the rest of our campus, which is the spot where Whitney always smoked when she decided to skip class. Sure enough, there she was. We saw the back of her red head; she was flicking her hair in the wind like me. A little stream of smoke drifted over to us, and my stomach jumped from being nervous. I fussed with my hair again. Abby pulled her brown hair out of its ponytail and shook her head, too.

Abby and I had always been a little afraid of Whitney, but I relaxed as we talked to her. Whitney was funny and didn't act like she was better than us. We joked more about classes and about our families. I was surprised when the warning bell for the next class rang. Luckily both Abby and I had gym, so we didn't have far to run.

'Are you going to Whitney's party on Friday night?' Abby asked as we walked to the bus stop after school. 'I think I'll be able to swing it. My dad is a bowling freak, and I'm pretty sure even he won't think I'll be able to get away with having sex on a bowling lane.'

'I'm going to try,' I said. 'I'll see what Granny says.' I hardly ever got to hang out with boys; Granny didn't approve of mixed-gender outings. I knew boys from my youth group, of course, but I didn't get to talk to them outside of church very often.

The key to talking to Granny, I knew, would be catching her in the right mood. Luckily it was only Tuesday, so I had some time if that night didn't work out in my favor. Sure enough, I could tell right when I got home that all was not peachy keen in our house. Granny and I lived in a pretty, big old house at the corner of Maple Lane. It was like something out of a storybook; doesn't it just sound like it? The house had been in our family since my great-great-grandpa built it, back when our family still had some of our Southern money. Granny had managed to hang onto it, even though we didn't have much money anymore. My grandpa had lost most of it during the Depression, but the house was important to our family.

Granny always said that it was breeding, not money, that made a Southerner. So we always kept the house, no matter what, even though property taxes sometimes made me think Granny was going to tear her own hair out. Granny had a hard life, and I know raising another child after hers were all grown up wasn't part of her plan. But I was all she had left.

Anyway, I could tell right away when I got home that things weren't good. Normally on a nice spring day like this Granny would have been waiting on the porch swing, the front door open to let the air into the house, with fresh iced tea ready for me. She liked to hear about my day. But the front door was shut tight and Granny wasn't waiting for me. I went inside and put my backpack and shoes in the front closet, and then I lifted a hand to make sure my braids were smooth, like they'd been that way all day. Granny's voice came from the kitchen; I couldn't hear what she was saying, but her voice was low and sharp. I banged a door or two before I went in to greet her, even though I knew Granny would be annoyed by how unladylike it was, to warn her I was coming.

The afternoon sun shone through the windows above the sink and lit up the yellow walls of the kitchen. Granny was seated at the large wooden table with the cordless phone in front of her. Her wrinkled hands rubbed her forehead and her shoulders before reaching to pat her tight grey bun, making sure it was in place before she looked up at me.

'How was school today, Sugar?' Granny looked tired, but she stood up and moved to the fridge to get our iced tea. I got the glasses and brought the cookie jar over to the table for easy reaching.

'It was fine,' I said. 'Miss Larson read part of my history essay aloud to the class, as an example.'

'That's wonderful,' Granny said, adding sugar to her tall glass of tea and stirring it with a long-handled spoon. 'Your daddy had a head for history himself.'

'How was your day, Granny?' I asked. 'You sounded a little upset when I walked inside.'

'Don't you worry about it,' Granny said. 'Just a little trouble with the bank.'

'Is there anything I can do to help?' I drained my glass of tea and took it to the sink to rinse.

'Nothing for you to worry about,' Granny said again. 'You best get upstairs and do your homework, now.'

'Yes, ma'am.' I left the kitchen and retrieved my backpack from the hall closet before going up to my room. It was the biggest upstairs bedroom: pink and white striped walls, with its own bath and a white balcony overlooking the backyard. Sometimes, in the summer, I stood out there in a long white nightgown and pretended I was Juliet.

Penny was laying at the foot of my bed, waiting for me. I pulled off my stockings and flounced on the bed next to her, burying my face in her long golden fur. Penny nosed me over and licked my face.

I couldn't talk to Granny that day, but I couldn't keep my secret to myself all night. I got a half an hour of phone time after dinner, but of course I had to talk in the kitchen or family room where Granny could keep an ear on my conversation, so it's not like I could tell anybody about the party. Penny, though, always kept all of my secrets. That's a great advantage of having a dog.

'Penny,' I whispered, 'you'll never guess what happened to me today.'

It turned out not to be too hard to get permission to go bowling, after all. At first Granny said no, but I pointed out that it was Whitney's gathering and that her daddy would be there the whole time. Granny likes Whitney's daddy—he's the lawyer who handled my grandpa's affairs after he died. Granny called him and found out there'd be at least three adult chaperones at all times, so I was allowed to go.

It was tough deciding what to wear that night. Naturally I didn't have any of the clothes I'd really have liked to wear: stylish clothes like the ones Abby and I poured over in the magazines she stole from her older sister, or even just cute ones from the mall like Whitney wore. Granny would inspect my outfit before I left, anyway, and there would be grownups everywhere to keep an eye on the buttons on our blouses. I walked around my room in frustration an hour before Abby's mom was supposed to pick me up, Penny's eyes following me back and forth as she curled on my bed.

'How am I supposed to make a cute outfit out of this?' I whispered to Penny, gesturing to the small pile of Wal-mart and Goodwill clothes I had tossed all over the floor. Penny yawned.

Ten minutes before Abby's mom arrived I had assembled myself into a pair of jeans, ballet flats, and my favorite secondhand navy blue button up cardigan (it was Hollister brand, but Granny didn't know that). I slipped my lip gloss in my pocket and smoothed out my long braid, planning to undo it as soon as I got to the bowling alley. I was ready for my very first non-church party.

Andrew was the first person I saw after I walked in the door. I had just pulled the hair tie off the end of my braid and was finger-combing my blonde hair over my shoulders in waves when I looked up and saw him watching me. He had messy red hair across his face and freckles across his nose. Abby saw him looking at me and pinched my arm.

'That's Andrew Schultz!' she whispered. 'He goes to my church.'

Lucky—or maybe unlucky—for me, Andrew wasn't shy. He came right up to Abby and me and asked if we wanted to be on his bowling team. I wasn't very good, but we had a lot of fun with Abby and Andrew trying to teach me. I learned a lot about Andrew—he was my age, he only lived three blocks away from my house, he had two dogs, and he wanted to be a doctor. He smiled a lot; I liked the way he smiled, especially when he was looking at me.

'Can I visit you?' he asked me right before we left.

'Visit me? I don't think I'm allowed boy visitors,' I said.

'I mean tonight,' he said. 'At your house. You said your room has a balcony.'

'Oh,' I said. 'Well... okay.'

I put on my fanciest nightgown when I got home that night, turned off the light, and waited on my bed. It seemed like hours before anything happened, but then I heard a plinking sound at the window – Andrew was tossing pebbles.

'Hi,' he said when I opened the doors and walked onto the balcony. 'Can I come up?'

'How?' I asked, looking at the smooth walls of our house.

'Oh,' he said. 'Um, well, my dad has a ladder in our shed. Hold on. I'll be right back.'

The first time Andrew visited, he asked if he could kiss me. The next time he asked if he could feel inside my nightgown. The third time, I asked him if I could see what his penis looked like. I bet you can just about guess what happened after that.

It was after the third meeting that Andrew said he loved me. He wrote me notes and passed them to Abby during church nights, and Abby gave them to me. I kept them in a special tin inside my locker, where Granny's vacuum or feather duster couldn't find them.

'Why couldn't you just have used a damn condom?' a nurse asked me when I was in labour with Mara, puking into a bucket and crying for my Granny. I tell you, some people don't know anything. My health class in school taught us that condoms have holes in them and most don't work, and that the material they're made of can make a lady's insides get itchy and red and then everybody will know what a sinner you are, and no one will talk to you anymore because you're a whore.

I wasn't even sure how babies were made. I knew it had something to do with sex, but I wasn't really sure what. All I knew was that you couldn't have a baby as long as the girl was on top, because of gravity. But I ended up with Mara anyway, so I guess I didn't know anything, either.

I found out about Mara three months after I started seeing Andrew. My period didn't come and didn't come. I tried not to worry, but when I started puking in the morning before school, I decided it was time to tell Abby. Abby talked to her big sister Libby, who bought me a pregnancy test that Abby smuggled to school. We skipped lunch that day and huddled together in the disability stall in the girls' room. I was so scared that I threw up twice waiting for the test to finish, and then I threw up again when I saw the two lines. Abby squeezed me something fierce and rubbed my back.

'You better tell Andrew,' she said.

I did tell Andrew, that night. I cried, and he cried with me, and he hugged me really tight and told me he loved me and would marry me. The next night is when he brought me the ring, which I hid inside one of my winter boots.

I was still trying to figure out how to tell Granny that I was getting married and going to have a baby when she found out anyway. She banged open the bathroom door one morning when I was quietly trying to puke before I left for school.

'Chloe, you're going to be late. What are you—oh, honey, are you sick?' Granny came over and felt my forehead. 'You don't feel warm. What hurts?'

'Just—just my tummy, Granny.' I said. Granny looked sharply at my face.

'Something is going on, here,' she said. 'What's the matter?'

'Nothing, really,' I said. 'I just have an upset tummy. Maybe it was something I ate?'

'Chloe Rebecca Stern, I can always tell when you're lying. What's wrong?' That's when I started crying and crying and couldn't stop. I told her the whole thing, all of it—all about Andrew and the puking and the period and the test and the ring and the wedding. Granny didn't say anything for a minute, and then she reached out and slapped me very hard across my face.

'After all I've done for you, and this is how you act?' she shouted. 'I thought I taught you better than that. What would your father say? I took you in and raised you myself and you turn out a common slut.' Then she sat down hard on the edge of the tub, one hand over her heart and the other reaching for the cross necklace that always hung around her neck. She cried for a long time.

When we were both all cried out, Granny wiped her face and then reached up to tighten her bun. She was back to being businesslike, going down to the kitchen to call a doctor and, as I found out later, a social worker who knew where she could send a girl like me.

The day I left Granny's house, she sat me down at the kitchen table and cut off my braids.

'I am so disappointed in you,' Granny cried as she cut. 'I failed your daddy in raising you.' She cut off all my long blonde hair up to my chin and then picked up my suitcase to drive me to the home where fallen girls go to have their babies.

That was my last day of being a girl. Now I'm a woman, I guess, and I can tell you it isn't much fun. Nobody at church will talk to me, Abby can't see me anymore, Andrew's parents keep him away from me and Mara. I could hear Mrs. Schultz's voice when Granny called to tell her the news: 'I'll be damned if some little tramp is going to ruin Andrew's future!' Mr. Landers watches me all the time, always telling me to pull up my stockings or button up my sweater more, even when it's a hot day. Mrs. Landers watches me around her husband and has me scrub a lot of toilets.

The only thing I have is the woods behind their house, the place I'm right now as I tell you this story. The Landers live on the edge of town, and a great big shady wood sprawls around right behind their backyard. It's tangled and thick, with fallen branches underfoot and roaming bushes and mosses creeping up the trunks of trees. I disappear in here whenever Mara is asleep and I don't have any chores to do, which isn't very often. Sometimes, when I can't sleep at night, I creep out here and stand by the edge of the trees. I love to vanish into the woods, where nobody can see me. When Mara is bigger, if I decide to keep her, I'm going to take her into the woods, too. I want her to learn how to be hidden and free, to keep something for herself away from the eyes of grownups. Even from me.

Return to Sender

Cynthia Rogerson

When his letter finally arrived, she didn't tear it open – though she wanted to. (This was the era before email, when letters could make your heart pound.) No, she swallowed her excitement and scolded her children in her usual tone of exasperation.

'Oh, for heaven's sake Wilma, you cannot go out dressed like that. Are you actually wanting to get pregnant?'

And:

'No, no, no Andrew. Did you really think I'd give my car keys to someone I gave birth to? Are you insane?'

No real anger in her voice, and the children responded with their usual rote sullenness, mumbling *sod you* as they slinked back upstairs.

The unopened letter from their father gained volume with every second it sat in her apron pocket. (This was also the era when all mothers wore aprons from the minute they got dressed to the minute before they sat down to a child-free dinner with their husbands. The pinnie period.) Any longer, and the letter would vibrate and perhaps even explode through the fabric like one of those IRA letter bombs. She waited for the slam of the front door as the children left for school, but even then she did not tear it open. She studied it, even lifted it to her nose for a sniff. It was one of his work envelopes, with his name and the London office address printed in the left top corner. The stamp was first class and his handwriting was more legible than usual. The ink was cheap – probably biro. She'd given him a nice fountain pen for Christmas; no doubt he'd left it behind.

She had no evidence of unfaithfulness. There'd been no unexplained lateness, or long blond hairs on his suit, or suspicious receipts in his pockets, or phone callers who mysteriously hung up when she answered. But still, he'd been acting strange lately. Energetic; happy in a frenzied way. Pre-occupied. He'd been walking differently too – as if he'd gone back in time, and was eighteen not forty eight. She put the kettle on to boil and then steamed open the letter. Slowly, slowly, she extracted the damp missive from the un-torn envelope.

Dear Edna: Please don't be angry.

Damn right she was angry. A two day business trip to London, evolving into a week-long silence, which (according to his secretary) was not due to being kidnapped, or drowning in the Thames, or suffering a drink-related injury to his writing hand, or...anything else she could make up.

I've been waiting to figure it all out. And yes, I am a coward.

I knew that!

Well, you knew that. I am not going to waffle any longer.

Oh please, waffle away. It's better than what you're probably about to tell me.

I am in love.

Christ.

I didn't mean this to happen. It just happened.

Like hell.

I am so sorry. Though I think we both know, our marriage died years ago.

Moron! Did you really think parenthood wouldn't change anything? Kids ruin everything. I knew you'd leave me one day because of them.

The kids have been the best thing in my life for the last decade. I was going to stay with you forever, because of them.

Silly me. Nothing to do with me, then. What about my chicken pie you claimed to adore? And that thing I do to you sometimes, after a bath when the kids are out? And that other thing I let you do to me, on your birthday last year?

But now I've met someone else. Please don't expect me to change my mind, I am never coming back to you.

Regretfully,

Archie

She stood up, then sat down, then stood again and paced round the room. She returned the letter to the envelope, sealed it up with spit, found a red pen and crossed out her name and address. She wrote: *Return to Sender!* across the front. She did this with her left hand, so her handwriting was not recognisable. Then she walked to the post box and popped it in.

She proceeded to treat the day like any other day, and all the days for the following week. This was not always easy, but nor was it as difficult as one might think. No person or thing reminded her of his letter, and it was surprisingly easy to be distracted by the usual things for entire minutes. Sleeping was not so easy, however, and she took to slugging whisky on and off all night like a baby with a bottle. This played havoc with her appearance in the morning, so she fabricated a virus that affected her eyes and balance. Her boss gave her the week off.

The second letter arrived and was promptly steamed open.

Edna: This is the second time I've written, but it was returned for some reason. So here goes, a second time. I have met someone else and I am not coming back to you. I am in love. Please explain to the children any way you like. I know they'll be angry, but they hate me anyway.

Good bye!

Archie

Again, she re-inserted the letter, scrawled with her left hand across the envelope: *Return to Sender* and popped it back in the post. Another week passed, during which she weaned herself off whisky, but found her appetite for food gone. Tying her apron on, she noticed her rib bones in a way she'd never noticed them before. Despite everything, she couldn't help but be pleased to find her waist again. Still, it was exhausting to be constantly panic-stricken, and worse – to have to conceal it. The skin under eyes was so dark now, she bought a cosmetic specifically for this problem. Doctor Dan's Miracle Vanishing Cream

When the third letter arrived, she did not bother opening it, just got out her red pen. Her heart was calmer, and hardly hammered at all posting it back to him. A month passed. The children did not seem to notice his absence, or indeed, her own emotional turmoil. She felt like a completely changed person, yet outwardly she was unchanged. Either that, or the children were utterly self-absorbed. She had to admit to a certain indifference towards them too, these days. Who were these gawky, smelly, rude creatures, and what had they done with those darling children in clean pyjamas?

She imagined her husband in his little love nest, trying to keep up the stamina and intensity all affairs demand. Not to mention the pretence of being a much nicer person than she (damn well) knew he was. It gave her a deep and secret pleasure, picturing him as his new lover wore him down. That woman, no doubt, would expect endless romantic gestures and presents and outings and sex late at night. She wouldn't yet know he preferred sex in the morning. He might begin to yearn for a lazy night in front of the telly, watching football and eating pizza. He'd order something with garlic and his farts would make her eyes water. She felt a curious protectiveness towards her wayward husband. Who would ever love him with the right mixture of contempt and need that she did? Meanwhile, she kept the house running smoothly, and bought some dresses to show off her new figure.

One day the children suddenly noticed.

'Hey, where's Dad? Wasn't he supposed to be back about now?'

'Your father? He was due home six weeks ago.'

'He was? Really?'

'But he's had to work longer in London.'

'Huh. Ok. Have you seen my new clogs?'

The letters finally stopped, and one Sunday, near Christmas – that season with a gravitational pull unknown to other months – he got out of a taxi and walked up to his front door. He was carrying the same small suitcase he'd left home with. She stopped breathing as she watched him from the kitchen window, dropping the tea towel she'd been holding. He didn't see her. As he approached, his face was blank. Then his eyes crinkled as if he was about to smile or he was thinking of something funny. Maybe he was practising looking happy. It was just a fleeting expression, and overall, she was struck at how old he looked. Old and flabby. He paused at the door, hand poised over the handle, then walked in while knocking. He opened his mouth when he saw her, then closed it. She stood in the kitchen doorway, feeling frozen and flat. Not at all how she'd imagined feeling. She wished with all her heart she was wearing something more flattering, but at least her hair was combed.

For a moment, neither spoke. Nor did they look directly at each other.

'Well! You're back!' she said casually, at last, and turned towards the kitchen as if needing to resume some chore. Slicing carrots or washing dishes.

'Sorry, Edna. I tried to...' He put his case down and followed her.

'No, no,' she interrupted, flapping her hands. 'Don't worry. The office told me about the, uh, about the new contract. I was expecting you around now.' She untied her apron automatically, then retied it.

'You were?'

'I bet you're exhausted.'

'Yeah, actually. I am knackered.'

'Cup of tea?'

'I'd love a cup of tea.'

She'd won, and all through dinner she felt celebratory. She insisted the children eat with them, and disconcertingly they conceded. They accepted his explanation of his absence, and no one asked any questions. The beef joint was perfect, and the potatoes were boiled then roasted in lard, just how he liked them. He fussed over making the gravy, then stood and carved the meat manfully. Her only regret was that she had no red wine, and they had to drink some cheap white.

They ate, cleaned up and watched the ten o'clock news from their usual chairs, the children having vanished upstairs. She admired the Christmas tree and hoped he would notice it too – though not notice she had not hung up those dreadful baubles from his mother. Arguing over choosing a tree and decorating it, had been their ritual for over two decades. The resulting tree had always been a disappointing compromise. She could not account for the way she'd missed that bickering this time, but this tree, her tree, was perfect.

After the news and a cup of tea, they brushed their teeth and went to bed, where he silently made love to her. She tried not to mind that he had some new moves. It was a relief to let go, even for a minute or two. When he turned to sleep, she curled up behind him as was her habit, and snaked her arm around his waist. He was not entirely familiar, but that was alright. It occurred to her there was an innocence to him now. She knew about his deception, but he was unaware of her own. She inhaled him, a combination of fart and Old Spice, and felt deeply grateful.

'My prodigal husband,' she whispered affectionately to his shoulder blades, then brushed them with her lips.

But he did not reply, and when his breathing became soft snoring, she found she could not sleep. She pulled away, lay on her back and thought about the way he hadn't commented on her smaller waist or the perfect Christmas tree. And this other woman – what was she doing right now? Was she also awake? Puzzled, angry, relieved? Was her pillow soaked in tears? Then Edna felt her presence suddenly and sharply, as if she'd joined them in bed.

Had, indeed, curled up on the other side of her husband, causing the mattress to dip a little. Edna slowed her own breathing and lay very still and felt very heavy. Her limbs had never felt heavier, as if the bed itself was sucking her down. She wondered if this was what dying felt like. But even so, she knew the sky would soon lighten, and they would rise and shower and she would spread marmite on his toast, and their lives, on the surface, would continue as normal.

Hiding

Malachy Tallack

My mother never liked this beard. It made me look scruffy, she said, 'like a tramp'. Sometimes she would look at me and shake her head in disappointment. 'You used to be so handsome', she'd say. But I was never handsome.

I grew it in my late twenties, not long before I moved to this house. I forget exactly why I first stopped shaving. Maybe just because I could. Or maybe because I wanted to hide myself a little, and a beard was the best I could do.

I wonder, now that I think of it, if my mother's disapproval had more to do with that act of concealment than with my scruffiness. After all, these whiskers hid from her the boy I once had been. They covered the cheeks she'd squeezed when I was a baby. They made me look like someone she didn't know, someone who didn't belong to her. I could understand if that was difficult.

But perhaps, too, my mother didn't like the white hairs that were woven in among the black of my beard. They were always there, those pale strands, long before I began to go grey on top; and I wonder if, in those threads, she saw herself undone. Perhaps this beard reminded her that she was getting old. I could understand that, too.

Now, nearly all my hairs are grey, and my mother is four years dead. She never liked my beard, but I kept it anyway. Until today.

I don't know quite what made me pick up the kitchen scissors this morning and bring them in to the bathroom. I went through to make my coffee first thing, then sat, as I always do, in the chair beside the window, opposite the stove. I was looking out – half looking, half thinking about nothing in particular – and enjoying the April sunshine on my skin. It faces east, that window, so it's the right place to sit at that time of the day. I can almost see the ocean from there, if I crane my neck to the north.

When my coffee was done and I was ready to go wash and dress, I already knew. I had decided without deciding. I took the scissors from the cutlery drawer and brought them to the bathroom. I laid a sheet of newspaper out over the sink to catch the hair, and I began to cut.

I do this sometimes – once a month at most, I guess. I snip and trim, just a little, to keep it under control, to stop myself from looking too wild. But this morning was different. This morning I was cutting close, laying the blades against my face and taking all I could take. Back and forth I went, cut after cut, enjoying the clean, crisp sound of the metal doing its work, and the sight of the grey clumps falling.

What was left when I was finished was a strange mess. On my cheeks there was not much more than stubble, with the pale skin visible beneath. But around my chin and neck, where it was harder to manoeuvre the blades, the hair was patchy and tufted. I stood and stared at myself in the mirror for a moment, postponing the final stage.

I have a razor in my bathroom cabinet: a blue, plastic, disposable thing. My son left it there the last time he came to visit. That was more than a year ago now, but it's not yet rusty. I took it out, together with the can of shaving gel, then I filled my palm and lathered the foam on my face. I made sure to cover everything, nice and thick, then I looked back at the mirror.

One beard was almost gone, and another was in its place. I was hidden again, this time beneath white sludge, like a melting Father Christmas, pathetic and ridiculous. I regretted, then, what I'd done. I wished back every curl of hair. My impetuousness, so unlike me, had been a mistake.

But I couldn't go back. At least not right away. And I couldn't leave it as it was. I had to continue and then to be patient, let it return in its own time. So I lifted the razor and began, drawing a long stripe from my left ear down towards my chin. Then again. I rinsed and shook the blade, then drew it once more over my cheek, upwards this time, the skin emerging clean, like a mowed, rolled lawn.

The first time I tried to shave I was fourteen years old, and what little hair I had on my face was soft and not yet in need of removal. But I was impatient. My father used a straight razor; I had watched him do it, and so I thought I knew how. Looking back, I suppose it was lucky I began on my cheek and not on my neck. It could have ended worse. The blade was sharp – he never let it be otherwise – and the cut was instant and deep: a two inch gash below my right ear, a gully of blood.

My mother found me on the bathroom floor, howling, my hand against my face. She cleaned me up and stopped the bleeding, then put everything back as it was meant to be. She wiped the sink and mopped the floor. But she couldn't hide the cut from my father. Later that evening, he hit me on the legs with the leather strop he used to sharpen the razor. No doubt he thought there was a kind of justice in that. 'Next time ask before you take my things!' he yelled, striking me across the back of each thigh. I suppose what he felt inside was something like concern, or perhaps even love; but it was a love indistinguishable from his rage.

Clearing the foam from my face with the blade, I see the scar emerge again for the first time in decades. The pale, smooth strip of skin almost surprises me, just as the memories of my father sometimes do. He lived only a few more months after that day. His heart, I think, could no longer contain all that anger. One day it just burst.

Wiping my hand over my bare cheeks and chin I feel exposed and uncomfortable. I don't want to look at myself anymore, so I turn my head away from the mirror. I miss my mother this morning – perhaps that's why I did it – and I even miss my father. You can't help these things, I guess. I put the razor in the bin beneath the sink, then step in to the shower.

Wild Air

Catriona Knapman

Moscow rushed over the Nile today like a new sort of winter.
Breathing truth down hot necks.
'I would have called you', she says. And she means it.
But she didn't and so *khalas*.

Here, God is remembered. There on the river, in the shivering road and in the wild air of African
winter.
'He would have come with you', she says. And it is true.
But he didn't and so *khalas*.

So, onwards, down the river, through the Southern bends of the city, towards
tufts of villages and the round
cracked toes of women who are
whole in their whole lives. Where they
bloom like flowers, crack
like thumbs and lick
their tongues, sweet as dates, over their words.

'You would have come before', she whispers.
And you would have.
But you didn't
and so, *khalas*.

Tutankhamun's Trumpets

Claire Quigley

Lucas

The watchmen's lanterns fail. The Cairo night
is snuffling round us, hot and dark as tombs
out in the desert. The dead see without sight:
they cluster in the corners of these rooms
moving on exhalations of my breath.
The sound conceals the scratch-tap of their tread,
these hollow men who know no rest, even in death.
A rasp of light, a candle flowers, easing my dread
at what we are about to do. The long
necks of the instruments stretched out, their mouths
fragile as glass blown from a furnace into song.
I close my eyes, but cannot still my doubts:
I saw one shatter just two days before;
fall in a cloud of silver curses to the floor.

Tappern

They give me the command to go
at nineteen hundred hours. I stand alone
in darkness while they cower. Like them, I know
the last man in my place saw silver blown
to shrapnel in his hands. I've heard them speak
of curses in the night, of how this land
can make the minds of even strong men weak
(and yes, my dreams are filled with blood and sand.)
At my feet, black snakes wind through the crypt
a sound-fuse to civilians waiting for the roar.
I hold the trumpet up, the whole length to my lips,
and blow three thousand years of silence from the core.
Then bugle-bright, a note burns through the wire:
some eldritch spark to set the world on fire.

Note: A pair of trumpets found in the tomb of Tutankhamun were played on a BBC radio broadcast aired on 16th April 1939 by a Bandsman called James Tappern. The program also featured Alfred Lucas, one of Howard Carter's original team. Legend suggested that the trumpets had 'Magical powers' and the ability to summon war.

Recital

Marianne Macrae

I am wearing a horse's head
and still you do not notice me.
The nail varnish on my toes matches
the mint-cream green of your t-shirt.
Neither of us are wearing socks.

I'm part of a much larger horse,
you'll see it soon;
handcrafted bamboo frames,
wrinkled with white tissue paper,
a chorus line of horse parts
all singing the same horse song.

Peeking through the curtains
I see you in the crowd, spilling a secret
to someone who isn't me.
Your face opens and closes like a drawstring bag
as we clip-clop on stage
for the opening number.

My horse head mouth does not move
but underneath it I am singing
with a mouth so wide and dark
I'm afraid of what will come out of it.

A Brief Incomplete History of Nuremberg

Gerry Loose

The sun is radiant this morning. Agathe Paul forgets how to say Middle East. She struggles and tries Near East, turns to me and asks – Sir, is this correct? She asks what comes to mind when I think of Nuremberg. Although I have been thinking of Dürer, she suggests the Nuremberg Trials. In the shop window, Dürer's hare is a fine shade of purple.

**

Katharina is almost three years old. In the garden the old bench is near collapse. Katharina has her hands clasped behind her back. Oh no! she says. And again. Oh no!

**

The Flesh Bridge between St Sebald and St Lorenz tells me: All things have a beginning and grow, but the ox upon whom you now look was never a calf.

**

On the Saturday Herr Wolf the butcher gives each of his customers a single red rose. This is to celebrate Mothering Sunday, when he is closed. His old father collects wild garlic every spring which Herr Wolf makes into a relish. Once, we lived in the countryside, he says.

**

It's the first garden get-together of the year for old friends. There is a crate of beer and a bonfire. Arno tends the fire with a new stainless steel long-handled spade. In the rising heat the newly leafed maple branches are swaying, coasting like a thousand bird wings. Michael will not leave until the fire is nothing but embers, safe. He was once a volunteer fire-fighter. Now he lives in a city-wall tower. The roof beams there are wooden, massive and exposed.

***

Max tells me ninety-eight per cent of wine is shit. He is unequivocal. It's a description he enjoys. He relishes the word, rolls it in his mouth even as I savour his champagne: his real naked champagne he tells me, zero dressage, pure Chardonnay, four years on lees in the bottle. Shit! he carefully articulates, once again. Max is not prosaic; his speech is grape-lyric, an ancient thing, clustered with the old vines of dusty hillsides. Passion. Here we used to drink lean, meagre and sour wines he says. No longer. Wine doesn't taste, wine gives a feeling. This – he gestures at his Larmandier-Bernier – has finesse, freshness, elegance. It is not able to be manipulated. We drink on. The taste of wine is just conventional; the secret for wine is the word; how it must be discussed and described. It is communication with yourself. Another gesture for a Mosel River Riesling: the lees is saying I can't ferment your sugar any more; I'm done. The Crianza has been two years in the bottle – Max is speaking fast – the Australians put sex, drugs and rock and roll in the glass. Europe has redefined its definition of what organic means. Forty-five of forty-eight inorganic additions to wine are now classified as organic. Ho. Ho. he says, very slowly. Another fling of the arm: here we have brioche, hazelnuts, brown butter. I have long since forgotten what we are drinking. Max is spectacular. He stares at me. I stare back. He speaks sadly: All this kind of shit has no relation to reality. Wine is communication.

**

Agnieszka arrived from Poland at the age of 16. She lodged with the nuns. At night, at lights out after prayers, she had to keep both hands above the blanket, flat, in clear view.

**

Can you tell me where Albrecht Dürer's grave is, she asks. I've lived in Nuremberg since I was born and I've never visited his grave.
Joachim von Sandrart, lying there more than four hundred years, lives to die, dies to live. Der du bist, der war ich. How many of us there are here. Anni Gerl, at ninety seven and just laid down, smiles. She is still hungry. She remembers those years. Hungry for life, hungry for rest. We walk to the grave together. There is a clump of shepherd's purse at its foot. It will rain.

**

Lumen de lumine:1698 and he still recalls the sun streaming through the plane trees by the river along Hallerwiese at noon, St Sebaldus' bells ringing clear in the distance. It resembles Charpentier's Midnight Mass. Light from light.

**

The hangman's hand is still intact, severed, under the axe, by Henkersteg near the wine store and the mature willow.

**

Carlos the Cultural Director says we're trying to use culture to revitalise communities. What Kristian the Creative Communicator-Coordinator does not say is when Capitalism bankrupts itself it turns to artists.

**

When Arnold was ten years old he met Herman Kesten at a reading. Shy and naive, he was the first to ask a question: Your name is Kesten; did you know Kessler? To which Kesten replied, yes; he is a friend. The ten-year-old and Kesten corresponded for many years. Arnold explains his work: the Nazis are only a pale frame. We must also deal with other types: for instance eco-fascists. There is one side with power and the other side with impotence. I deal with components of a certain tradition. The Arc of Triumph as a tank. The old language of architecture was highly symbolic. It's hard to remain a pessimist. I deal with war and military rituals with irony; but what is the spectator seeing? Pacasmayo, Paranagua, Kingston, Trapezunt, en transito, in Kraftshof read the zinc stencils in his studio.

**

My taxi driver, from Eritrea, will not believe there is snow now, in May, in Scotland. That's the North Pole, he says. He asks if Scotland is part of the United Kingdom. Nor will he believe the police in Scotland do not routinely carry guns. He can't drop me off in front of the station, it's not allowed. The Bavarian Police are very strong, he says. It's the Feast of the Ascension, a holy day of obligation.

**

The elderly woman with the dog will not direct me to the Underground station, but instead takes my arm and leads me there. Her grey-muzzled dog pauses at every tree and each lamp-post. She pauses. There are other dog walkers at this early hour and she keeps her shambling dog on a short lead. You must take care with dogs, she says. If you have a dog you know lots of people. The dog sniffs at the base of a lime tree. I can't tell her I'm in a hurry. The sky is unclouded. The sun warms her, the old dog and me.

**

The Mayor, in his second term of office, tells me that politics on a local level has a special place in democracy: If I go to the market and buy vegetables the people speak to me.

**

The coffee maker, buyer and blender, discusses the origins of his coffee and the rules of how to make the best of his beans.

The Artist, in a red jacket, orange trousers, purple shoes and a lime tee shirt poses in front of his painting. It's a painting of his ex who was always late. I count the incorporation of sixty-six clocks. The tee shirt maker was a graphic designer. She learned her transfer techniques from Japanese methods.

Outside the vintage shop the angel spits water unendingly into the fountain.

In their short avenue, Willie, Ellen and Elisabet each tend an individual plane tree.

Shadows grow.

**

Herr Wolf, the butcher, arranges a cooking competition between the Mayor and a Conservative.

**

Small children skip across Spitalgasse. A man in green shoes spins a red ball.

Everywhere poplar seeds on air drift into shafts of sun.

**

The doorman has volunteered for Blaue Nacht. He is seventy one years old, yes. He has a son of fifty three. He only gave up football last year because of a shoulder injury. Now he takes part in the Senior Olympics, has been a finalist many times. The crowd becomes pressing and is sweeping me into the House of the Holy Ghost. Parting, we shake hands, thumbs clasped. Inside there is a tray of M&M packets and prosecco for guests.

**

Are you looking for the toilet? Come with me says a man inside the café on Bergstrasse. Where are you from he asks; and Excuse me, as he delicately breaks wind. Tell the Czech and Polish at your table this is unique.

**

Up late, the wee girl runs wide eyed. Mama! Mama! she says and her long white dress is clean against the blue skirt of her mother as she hugs her mother's legs, for the sheer love of childhood, of the late night, of spring and grown up voices all along the street.

**

To Trude's secret delight Bayern did not win the match against Chelsea.

**

Pia, at seven, knows it's the headlights of cars in the street two storeys down making the lit-up shapes of windows on the white ceiling, but she doesn't know how. The window patterns sweep left to right and right to left, growing longer as they reach the walls, where they disappear. The best, the slowest, are the ones from right to left. When it happens both ways together, it's too fast, like scuttling spiders. It's an enchantment each night that sends her to sleep. She might sleep for a hundred years.

**

He accepts the archaeology of his dreams, with the more recent at the top. Here and there, fault lines. Those old dreams below the surface fractured, broken, compressed.

**

Oh, and Olof forgot the clouds: cumulus, piling to the east beyond vision.

**

Hanne's fingers are long. They caress the mushrooms they are slicing with the wooden-handled knife.

**

The white pigeon pecks between the granite setts among the blown blossom under the Robinia trees in Hans Sachs Platz. The bird is not a symbol.

**

The Editor-in-Chief says this town has some ugly parts. He wanted to say this before. His dear old mother-in-law, who's eighty-five, sometimes forgets his name. At the editorial conference, body language and lack of eye contact tell a different, unreadable, story. The paper has sixty journalists who pray for the publisher every day.

**

The white pigeon flutters to the left as Arnold's expensive bike comes too close. The artist does not see the bird, one of many.

**

Effi did her Masters in Manchester, She says she's just quit her job as a magazine journalist because she can't get on with her boss, whose partner in any case owns the magazine. She's fluent and damning in her appraisal of her boss. As a waiter, her other job in Hans Sachs Platz, she handles all orders with grace and humour.

**

The white pigeon is back, early.

**

The Historian says the beginning was in 1918. The elite could not accept defeat. Architecture was a symbol of intended world rule. The idea was to fill the arenas, the stadiums with thousands. The US Ambassador visited in 1938 and approved of this plan. That year, Adolf Hitler announced the intention to invade Czechoslovakia. The investigation into the past is to ensure such things can never happen again.

**

He sees the unfinished Nazi Congress Hall, intended to hold fifty thousand folk, slowly being reclaimed by trees and by Dürer's Great Lawn. Leaving the Hall, his unconscious leads him to hum Handel's aria from Judas Maccabaeus 'See the conqu'ring hero come'. Outside, the benches, in full sun, are built high. The women swing their legs like young girls.

**

The wall speaks: Nvllvm crimen, nvlla poena sine lege – kein Verbrechen, keine Strafe ohne Gesetz. No crime, no punishment, without law.

**

Angelika was young, a freelance journalist, just starting out. In 1985, she sat in the Press seat inside Nuremberg Court 600 for yet another Nazi trial of an insignificant but murderous Party member.

**

The white pigeon says a tree is a tree is a tree.

**

The Tavern Choir sings in the darkening garden behind Bucherstrasse.
There is a bottle for them each of white Franconian wine. A salad. The singing is spontaneous: they are four friends and have been at practice in the flat upstairs. They laugh and sing. The stars are in the sky above the rooftops. There is no audience. Bats flit above the trees.

**

The Thai woman lifts crates of drinks for the cafe two at a time from the boot of the car. She shifts one to her left hand, keeping one in her right and swings them both up the five sandstone steps to the back door of the café where she works. The sun is hot already. A bunch of keys swings from a long cord at her belt and bangs her knees. She does not pause at all, now bringing empty crates from inside the cafe to the car. A tram passes up the hill.

**

The white pigeon says: Albrecht, you never really look at birds. Take your engraving for the Apocalypse – where the angels have better wings than that odd eagle, who's saying ~*bebebe* – what's that? You know the one: in the Seven Trumpets in the Secret Revelation of St John – the Apocalypse at the End of Time. Have you never seen a dove feather flutter down from a lime tree?

**

Outside the Convent the nun has laid a table from which she sells Asterix comics. There is an honesty box.

**

Floods of fallen blossoms line the side streets.

**

The men sitting outside Franco's drinking coffee and white wine at noon are getting on. Their hair is thinning, swept back. There are ear-rings, two tone shoes. As they leave, one or two at a time, they hitch up their trousers. Each one lights a cigarette. The world is still here.

Certainty, times three (x3)

Jim Ferguson

are you being certified
is your planet made of stew
are you being crucified
cause the rent is overdue

are you singing very loudly
in the supermarket queue
people standing all around
they look at anything but you

*

hard work's no easy
remember I don't work,
that's a famous Scottish saying,
I don't remember work

haha! yes you do, you job-seek full-time
you're working every single casual day,
even when you're not working
you are working, yeah,
                    oh fuck aye,
                            'we have a friendly little course to send you to'

*

earth's not made of concrete
there's a lack of absolute
acid bus with wheels of clay
pulls-up fast and bears us all away

crocodile is out the river
hugs your stinking feet
jail flesh in the watery Seine
sing: *rentrer a la maison*

I see you're looking wonderful tonight
returning home, move back up river
gods and goddesses all,
feet not clay, feet not clay

homeland does as homeland do
clerks of death,
their charges too, cry:
rentrer a la maison

51' 08"

Iain Morrison (with thanks to Colin Herd)

So there was a point to this
what were we talking about before I brought up Star Trek?
Longing, things that you desire, transferring,
and you said you can like things that you didn't like beforehand
so I presumed that you were gonna say something about Star Trek being something you didn't like
beforehand but now that you do...
Yeah that was part of it, but there was also a specific thing from an episode of Star Trek that I was
thinking about in that way
I mean that's such a Star Trek thing, isn't it
I mean you mention sex and Star Trek and I'm immediately thinking of Deanna Troy
who was just sex in Star Trek
She was amazing I mean, she what an amazing woman, a everybody
right you know everybody me yeah but also
I mean yes. We watched this episode the other day where
she was like and her mother too for that matter. Do you remember her mother? I don't think I
know her mother
Like there was a hilarious episode where she had to get married naked because that's what the
Betazoids did
and like her husband wasn't up for it and then
Oh well that is so Betazoid isn't it? That's that's that's I mean I
this isn't what I was meaning, but Deanna Troy that is she can feel what you feel
Yes, yes she can
yeah and actually
Cos she can sense that you're playing up for the recording
and do you know what, part of my feeling
[laughter]
Which I'm not, nor are you I hope
Em but part of my feeling about love and desire does come from Betazoids on Star Trek,
my understanding of longing and sex and sensuality comes from Deanna Troy.
Do you remember that other episode where
who was having a relationship with who hang on, right
Beverley Beverley Dr Beverley...who did she, Crusher, Crusher, was she who was she having a
relationship with?
Picard

Oh fuck, it wasn't her then

There was one episode where

but maybe someone else at some point

someone died but their brain went into someone parasitic alien's body, next gen?

who was a different gender or something, and then then the, and they couldn't be with them

because actually the gender thing was too hard for them

even though it was the same person, Mmm, I can't remember.

I f..., I might try and find that one tonight

I feel like, I feel like it was Beverley Crusher when she was having a time off

cos she was never *formally* with Picard

no no no, they were just on the same wavelength yeah yeah yeah yeah

I think it was a time when she was with someone else

I think the someone else went into Riker's body and that was too much for her

or after that

yeah

no she coped she coped with Riker's body, cos he was a man

but then it went into somebody else's body who was a woman like

Have you Natasha Yar or something seen the one where they all go to children?

No

So like Picard, right who is it

Picard is a child, and then some other minor characters

oh and Whoopi Goldberg, Guinan, Guinan is a child. Loved her

Daylight Robbery

Ross Wilson

'Junkie bastard broke in,
broad daylight. Can ye imagine?
Tried tae wrench the door wi a crowbar,
then took a brick tae the windae.'
I imagined a face reflected in glass,
a brick smashing features like stone
shattering calm water in a loch,
affecting everyone within
the rippling of its concentric span.
The glass house would have been
much easier to break in had the robber seen
any value between its panes.
As my neighbour went on,
I remembered something
a pal once said, 'ken where the sayin
daylight robbery comes fae?
Windae tax. Imagine piyin fir sunshine!'
No sun, where's the light a bairn's
brain will grow?
But why would my neighbour
contemplate talk of nature and nurture?
He was the victim here.
'It makes ye wonder,' I began,
'what drives a man...'
'*They* make thir ayn decisions.
Wiv aw choices: some work so
they can afford keys tae enter rooms
thiv bought; ithirs think bricks acceptable
tae open doors thiv closed oan thirsel.'
It dawned on me then
I didn't even know his name.

How long had we lived in the same
building? 'Hope they get him,'
I said, opening my door and reaching down
for a letter I was soon to discover
concerned my spare bedroom.

Montmartre

Philip Miller

I

I went to bang my head off the wall,
But it was hessian, matting and gall.

I went to looks for knives.
But she had hidden them all

and left plastic children's tubs.
The kettle would not boil.

He went into the yellow air of the mall.
Dildos racked in the sex shop like clubs.

At the church he spent 100 Euros on candles.
He gave his kebab to the tramp's spaniel.

II

The city is not asleep.
Orange haze. Men huddled, and lights weeping
between trees, befuddled doorways, the ochre air.
In the inundations, they once carried each other there—
through flooded boulevards, man on man, tethered.
At Rue San Dominique a crowd of washed faces gathered.

In the cork lie baffled constellations.
At the cash point, a soft faced cutpurse –
one hand behind his back – gave instructions
to deceive and ran away. I punched him, it hurt.
He dropped to the tiles and slept. Or worse.
And the funicular is steadfast, stuck
on the ascent to the Sacre-Coeur.

The Robert Pattinson Sequence

Andrew Blair

Moon Pioneer

When Robert Pattinson was quite young
He entered a Blue Peter competition
To explain what the moon was

In those days, oh
The moon!
It was the source of much speculation

The winner would have their explanation enshrined As the best
Possible one
At the time.

The runners up would receive
Nine mountain bikes each
Two hats
And a badge much coveted (
Much
Much coveted)

Robert Pattinson sprawled childishly by the window -Eyes wide, heels kicking
Night sky beckoning -
And invented the moon

Childhood

Robert Pattinson did not go to the funeral.
The deceased had not told him
They were mortal

A brief interlude in the present day

Robert Pattinson is at a party
He knows he is talking about himself

Retail Therapy

Robert Pattinson is in Bed
Bath
And Beyond
Looking for existential revelations

Colour Blind People React to Gardens

Robert Pattinson
Lives in the hope of becoming
A symbol
Simple
Shorn
Purified and free
From sleepless flaws
Lacking complexity
Despite his success
The concept lingers

The concept lingers
Despite his success
Lacking complexity
From sleepless flaws
Purified and free
Shorn
Simple
A symbol
Lives in the hope of
becoming
Robert Pattinson

The Privilege of Dreamers

Robert Pattinson refuses to define freedom
He dreams

That he is asleep
And dreaming
In such dreams

Robert Pattinson steps faintly off the ground
Arcs
Peddles

Frightened Rabbit

Robert Pattinson's friend is a journalist But
he's not that bad
Robert Pattinson's friend has sent him this

Email from his iPad
Robert Pattinson had wanted to know

What people thought of his life

Nothing
Propels his dream body
Over naïve, defiant roads   And so Robert Pattinson asked to find out
Rolling nowhere
Forever
In place
Robert Pattinson believes   What the papers would say when he died
Interpreting this would
In reality   Robert Pattinson's obituary uses a picture of
                                             his face

Be hypocritical   A still from the film *Twilight*
For all he knows   Robert Pattinson's obituary has a blank
                                             space
The idea was here first   After the words 'is survived by.'

In conclusion

Robert Pattinson never asked to be made, with such limited purpose. There is nothing he can do on this earth but damage. When Robert Pattinson looks at a gun he thinks 'We are the same.'

Robert Pattinson believes western civilisation is fine if you just turn your brain off, if you don't think about it.
It wasn't made for critics, he says.

Robert Pattinson is in a lift with some strangers. He always asks 'Are we young now?' just before the doors open.

Robert Pattinson lost a loved one, and the pain grew so great he had someone cut it out of his heart. He was surprised at how small it was.

Robert Pattinson hates it when poets do a load of jokes and then undercut it with abrupt pathos.

He hates when his name doesn't belong to him, when it becomes white noise.
He sees dead people all the time
If he closes his eyes he asks if he sees the inside of his lids, and if this still counts.

Robert Pattinson hates it when poets

A rainy day. The trousers Robert Pattinson was wearing the night the star fell are in the wash.

☞

Robert Pattinson sees his old diaries in the rainfall. He almost doesn't notice the piece of his heart in them, because it's so small.

Robert Pattinson believes sleep is a simulation of death. He believes that the world ends every day as soon as your eyes close and sleep takes hold.

With a start Robert Pattinson realises - as of 17/04/16 - he has survived 10,568 apocalypses.

Robert Pattinson dislikes contrived segués. He believes that people should emerge from despair organically.

Robert Pattinson sees dead people resting patiently on his bookshelves and finds it calming

Ideas come gently and go nowhere

Robert Pattinson knows he will live on in hearts and minds because not only is he loved, but also there are several million branded products bearing his likeness and name.

Really isn't that all any artist can ask for?

His days will become Batman
His nights will persist
Books only end if you let them
It's easier
But there are blank sheets of paper between the text and the covers
And more paper outwith
You simply aren't trying

Keep warm
Robert Pattinson will become fuel
Still
You will never see the light disappear
From his eyes.

Stela

Mikhail Mavrotheris

%   —

?

,

.

         .   ! thank you so much

      –'   you saved   (saves me   )

       - ,   ,

—   — ,   ,

         .   ... haha

     —   —   ,

      —   - ing <u>ολλ τηε ςαυ</u>

       ,   . I love grammar. (

   ,   )–   I love grammar. (χιχ χιχ Χιχ–

XA<u>X</u>(0( ))),   music of grammar.   "

    "   (   )   )   )))'   .

                  —   .

       9 or 10   , or

   ,   (((( )))),   ,

   .   ???!

                    γιυ τιυ οτελα (')

                  τοθ μ. μ. μαραβοθ

Στέλα (' '   "λ'   "('   '   ' ''   ))

Blue Monday
(Disco Biscuits #3)

Andy Jackson

We are reading from the bible of the blues today,
the morning after like a remix of the night before,
the needle swinging back to the start to play
the album through again. There must be more
than this; the same old rhythms every week,
a rehash of the usual songs, an inoffensive curse
of days, euphoric flourishes replaced by bleak
chords and dissonance, all chorus and no verse.
Yet with a word from you I could be swayed
into believing what my mind says can't be so;
that the outro of the final song will never fade,
that balloons or odd-shaped clouds are really UFOs.
Like grains of sugar scattered on a morning frost,
there if you're looking, but just as easily lost.

Methane

Paul Walton

So I'm on the footbridge by the bbc and I've stopped to look because the river surface is bubbling small bubbles all over. That has to be methane gas escaping from the riverbed I think. Old leaves. And god knows whatelse. And this guy who stopped and is looking too says that's methane gas escaping from the river bed. I say why now, why today, and he says it's because the flow of the river is slow today and that lets the methane escape and I say but what if it's just that the river is low and more shallow, so there's less weight of water on the gas. He says no it's the flow rate, I work in fluid engineering. I say righto then. Are you sure it's not more about the depth and he says no I think flow rate is the more important determinant of bubbling. And then he says no hangon mibby you're right. Yeah it's depth thats more important. We are both nodding cheerio. The Clyde does not look either slow or shallow today.

Pulling Away

Paul Foy

There was sunshine and there was heat. There would have been birdsong but I couldn't hear it.

There was just me and the old lady on the carriage. Then there was just me when she got off.

Well, sort of just me. And sort of 'got off'. Even if you're as far on in your miserable years as she was, thinking it's a steady but predictable decline from now on, life can still come at you with the steel toecaps on.

The train pulled into the station and up she got. I was watching her. Usually it's who's getting on that interests me. Would there'd be some kid who'd glance at me now and again, like that's all it was – a glance. Or maybe a group of kids that I'd hope would not be caring about me, all of them laughing too loud. Look at us, but you'd better not look at us. My trouble was I could never stop looking. What wasn't there not to look at? They were a different species. Some scientist – I thought – should dissect them. Chop them up and put the bits in a jar. Preferable a jam jar with some of the jam still in, and then you could leave it out in the back garden near the bins and wasps would crawl in and get stuck. And if you wanted – and your parents weren't around – you could take the jar to the kitchen sink and watch as the little stripy, stinging bastards drowned.

When she – this old lady, like a spruced up, face painted hag from a fairy tale – was getting up out of her seat she looked at me and smiled, lipstick on the ends of her teeth. I didn't smile back. I was disgusted at all the grunting noises she was making, saying 'Ah dear' and sighing to let me know what an effort it was for her. I couldn't see the point in her smiling. Was I meant to feel sorry for her or something? Or to understand what it was like for her? How could I possibly do that?

But I kept watching her, keeping my face blank, like one of those white mime masks you can buy in the cheap shops these days. The idea was to look, but at the same time to get the message across: I'm not interested in someone like you, with your skin like paper that's got wet and then dried up again. And look at your bones sticking through it, the bits that aren't hanging down and jiggling about. I thought about what she probably looked like under her clothes, those tits of hers lying flat against her ribs with probably big brown nipples that had lost all interest for anyone. And folds of skin below her belly button, hanging down like they're trying to cover that smelly old crack of hers that's only good now for dribbling out piss. Imagine seeing that in the mirror every morning before you went for your shower. I was thinking of how people joked about how old people never washed enough and that's why they smell of wee. Looking at her I thought that I'd rather smell than have to take my clothes off day after day and see how repulsive I'd become.

And then the train stopped and did a little wobble, which made the old woman wobble, and there was a big hiss as the automatic doors opened to let her out. She did another look back at me – not smiling this time but looking puzzled or worried or something – then concentrated really hard on putting her feet down on the little step, probably nervous she would miss it and get her bone-yard ankle caught down there between the train and the platform. If she did that she'd fall and her shin bone would probably just snap like a dried up wishbone. I wondered if you could make a wish if that happened.

That's not what happened.

It was just a small step down from the train but she was like a little toddler trying to get onto the platform. She put one foot down and looked like she was going to fall so she stuck her arm out, holding onto the rail inside the doors, that skinny wrist sticking out from her coat that was too warm for a day like it was, claw-like fingers at the end of her hand, all gnarly and sore looking, probably from arthritis or something. When you see something like that you can't help thinking about some of the things hands like that might have done in the past. Like did they play the piano or violin? Did they move all gracefully and make tunes that make you confused because you don't know if you're feeling happy or sad; or perhaps they drew really good drawings and paintings, or made jewellery out of sea glass that they collected on holiday. Or maybe they had done dirty things to boys or even dirty things to other women. But you tried not to think about these things because you didn't like the way they made you feel.

I felt my stomach go all tight and hurting so I finally managed to look away, out the window at the grass turning yellow on a hill going up from the station on the far side of the track. I can only think now how it was lucky for her that I had forgot to charge my phone, otherwise I would have had my earphones in listening to Die Antwoord or some dangerous shit like that and probably not have even heard her.

Before you knew what was happening there was a big hissing sound again as the doors closed and then it was just me on my own as nobody else had got on and the old lady had got off.

Tried to get off, but never quite made it.

I heard her going 'Oh! Oh! Oh!' which I thought was really stupid because she should have been screaming something like, 'Will somebody fucking do something before I fucking die!' But even when Death is pissing itself at the state you've got yourself into, old ladies can still manage to be polite even though they're totally shitting themselves. You've got to give them that.

So what happened was, her arm was still inside the carriage when the automatic doors slid together and grabbed her, and because the train guard couldn't have been doing his job properly and didn't see her, the train pulled away and she was getting pulled along with it, her wasted legs trying to run along to keep up. It was like something Mr Bean would do, but I wasn't laughing at it like maybe I was supposed to, but I guess I just wasn't in on the joke.

Or perhaps it was because the joke was really on me.

Going to help her the way I did.

I suppose that was instinct or something that got me by the scruff of the neck, making me do it. And it was the weirdest thing, looking at her. She reminded me of a laboratory animal that has had perfume poured into its eyes to see how it likes it – and, of course, it isn't going to like it one bit. Why would it?

So I'd grabbed hold of the arm trapped in the door and pulled as hard as I could – with all my might! – and she somehow have managed to scramble her legs up onto the step that was just outside the door. Imagine if she hadn't done that? She'd have slid down and down until her feet started dragging along the ground, getting smashed to bits and all bloody and she'd have screamed and screamed, getting pulled further and further away from me until her hand popped away from mine and she'd have been gone. But that didn't happen, she didn't even scream. Which amazed me, that even when you're really ancient and past it and should really just accept your fate, an old woman like that could still have the strength to fight on to stay alive the way she did.

There wasn't really much for me to do once the train got really moving, except look at the face of pure terror outside the glass. Or should it be 'Stared into the face of pure terrified'? Because it's not like she was a demon or anything like that. She was just totally bricking it, though I didn't like the way she kept her eyes on me, like she was thinking that as long as she did that and not look away then I wouldn't let go of her.

Then again...

Perhaps she was a demon after all, because she managed to fill me with the sort of fear I'd never felt before. Is that what happens to you when you grow old? You become monstrous, even if you don't even know it? Even when you were getting burned as a witch, you didn't know that you had fallen in with the Devil? When the dwarves are hunting you down because you're a minging old bitch that tried to destroy beauty? You can't always rely on good manners to save you.

It was my terror that saved her.

Because I wanted to let her go. Down the track a bit, a few minutes before the train reached the next station – though probably an eternity for the old bint – just past the bowling green full of more old people in white, there's a tunnel. And when the train went through it and out of the sunlight I saw the most horrifying thing I'd ever seen in my life. Real pit of the stomach, nerve shredding, nearly crapping yourself scary. Right there in the dark, neither inside or out.

You go into a tunnel on a hot sunny day and you feel a bit colder. You don't feel like your blood is freezing, that your eyes are going to split and burst, but that's what the reflection I saw did to me.

There was me in the glass, arms out in front of me holding the reptile wrist of an arm, like I'm pulling a weed out of the ground. But there's a trick being played on me. A trick of the light, because it's my body but it's not my face. Instead it's the face of the old lady, right there on top of my neck where mine should be. And because this is being done to me – because the old witch has done this to me – it's like my body has been stolen from me as well, all control gone, and not just from the one in the reflection, but the one that my mind is trapped in. I want to let the old lady fall, but instead my grip tightens and I can't even think straight, my thoughts are coming from nowhere, I don't know where they're coming from or where they're going. No, I do know where they are going – out that door, zooming through space and time, scraping against the wall of the tunnel, screaming into madness and nothingness, except that I can't scream, there's no control, I can't stop my fingers clamping tighter, no control and no point. No point. There I am. I'm that old lady, wanting to let go of this disgusting thing mirrored back at me yet all my muscles and tendons and nerves are working against me to save a life that has no right to claim from me what it is taking. It's theft. Nothing but theft. Theft is all there is for us.

And then we're out the tunnel and the old lady is gone. And I'm gone too.

It's white.

That's all there is.

White.

No shape, no feeling, no sound, not even pain. Just white. I try to flap my arms like a bird to see if I can get some feeling back into them, but I have no arms. I want to twirl round and round to make myself dizzy and sick, but there's nothing of me to twirl. It's not white mist. There's no mist to twirl. There are no thoughts in my head to twirl. Do I feel the panic building up in me? How can I when there's no more me. There never was a me and there will never be a me. There's not even nothing left because there never was anything.

Just nothing from nothing.

And then I'm back.

Do I know where I've been? I don't. All I know is that I'm here, but there's no relief. I'm not even confused – what just happened to me made sense. In that moment – if you can call it a moment – lack of sense was the only thing that had ever made sense; and if I could, wherever I had gone, I would have stayed there forever. But I can't, because there's a situation here and I'm jolted right back into it and the white light has become a dream, and all dreams want to do is race to get away from you. Clickety-clackety chugga chugga clickety-clackety chugga chugga clickety-chlackety chugga chugga…

There's pain.

My fingers are clenched so agonisingly tight they've seized up. My nails must be digging right into the loose flesh beneath the sleeves of the purple woollen coat, but I don't suppose she's caring too much about that. Does she even know that we're heading into the station? That unless she has a heart attack or stroke or something she's going to make it – a dribbling extension to her days?

It's now that panic starts to infect me as the train slows and I see people running alongside it as it hisses to a stop. Bodies crowd round the old lady, hands reaching out to take hold of her, to make sure she doesn't fall. To relieve me of my burden. Except that when the doors finally hissed open I still have hold of her. I need someone to take my fingers and straighten them out for me – you'd have thought I was the one that was arthritic.

Once I was free of her I sat down and tried to get all composed again, and it was good that the old lady fainted once she was brought inside the carriage again as everyone wanted to help support her and get her seated, all focus away from me. Again I was watching, even though I just wanted them to take her away and let the train take me to where I was going so that I could start trying to forget what had happened. Why did they even have to bring her inside the train again? Couldn't they just take her to the station waiting room and phone an ambulance or something and everyone get on with it.

The trouble was, the way she fainted was comical – in a weird and twisted sort of way – and I almost burst out laughing.

She was lifted bodily off the step and placed down on her feet.

'Oh, that was terrible,' she said, in a pathetic little old lady voice, and then she did the sort of swoon you would expect a bad actor to do. She even did the bit where she put the back of her hand to her forehead before falling back into the arms of a burly big bloke who acted a lot more gentle than he looked.

What could I do but put my face in my hands, making a snuffling noise that someone must have mistook for crying.

'Are you all right?' I was asked.

Another little squeal came out of my mouth, high pitched and embarrassing, and then the old lady came round and started going on about how I was wonderful, I had saved her life, and then everyone was looking at me – and someone said he was phoning a newspaper - and I had to stick my head down on my knees as I was going to have an hysterical fit or something, but not because this was funny ha! ha! but because I wanted to just be left alone, and I wanted to not be some wonderful little teenager that had done something amazing.

I got up and boltd out of the train, then along to the back of the train, down onto the track, then I ran along it as fast as I could, back the way we had just come. There was shouting behind me, but I wasn't interested in it. I was headed to the point, the bridge between light and dark because that was where the white was. That is where the white is. But try as I might, with tears flowing from my eyes, crying properly now, the white hid from me. It hid from me. Why reveal itself and then hide itself?

I realised something then:

That it wasn't my white. The colours still wanted me. The clickety-clackety chugga chugga racing forward still wanted me. But I didn't want them. Who did they think they were, trying to lay a claim to me?

It was a hot sunny day and I could hear the birdsong, echoing about in the mouth of the tunnel and I passed out. Like stupid old woman I fainted. And as I fell I heard voices around me and I felt the hands grasp my arms, but I didn't care about them because I wanted the white to come to me, but it wouldn't.

There was only darkness.

Darkness on a bright summer day.

There was darkness and it was cold. I could hear the birdsong.

Epicentre

Stobo

Something has happened,
– you are aware of that;
something ruptured and crushed
the atmosphere around you.
A symphony mute
under a score of muffled weeping,
tears and faces in sleeves –
but mostly it is noiseless,
a shock vacuum,
emptier than all space
but for an ink blot blackness
spreading from its centre
absorbing all around it,
levelling the interconnected world,
throttling your spirit.
You await the CPR
for your flatlining soul.

Women

Tessa Berring

Who dont know gentleness,
long to make blancmange;
to tip it down the necks
of comfortable funnels,
whispering words like
buttocks and fandango.

I Will Haud Ye

George T Watt

I will haud ye fan the nicht is snell
an sterns are twinkle in the lift,
a fu muin glimmin ower the yell
an yon caul nor-wund threitnin drift.

I will haud ye ticht an fast,
nae thocht o ither will cam atween,
the cranruech caul micht tent its blast
but I will guard agin its scheme.

I will ner be caul or blate,
tho ice micht hairden yird an burn,
the Arctic blast micht wrass the slate
but I'll be thare at ilka turn.

I will haud ye trui an dree
tae warm the cauldest winter nicht,
ma hert's ease ye gae tae me,
nae Arctic snaws can mak me licht.

Miscarriage

Lauren Pope

I'm told
the moonstone
I carried
in the palm
of my hand
could not alone
will a living thing
to term,

and the eggs
consumed
upside down
on a Sunday
once held
the same possibility
for which I grieve.

Sometimes things
that do not exist
are real –
the way my ears
hear Etta James
sing 'Cadillac'
not 'At Last,'
or how the opening
acoustics
to Little Wing
are, to me, a mimesis
of drowning.

Announce this: today,
the colour of failure
is the robin's
sanguine throat.

Robbie and the Grizzly Bear

Leonie M Dunlop

You telt me aboot thon time at school
when you foond your grizzly bear.

Push came tae shove
and that shove saw you birled intae the ring of boys.
Your hands, nimble fingers quick at tying knots for fishing flies
curled into hard wee fists
for the fight.

Jabbin, reelin them in,
dartin roond the bigger boys
like a minnow roond stanes in a rock pool.
Sleekit wee eel.
All at once takin every trick
from baith the fish and the fisher.

Little on mickle
wi knuckles raised tae your chin
you'd foond that bear
and boy could he roar!

A whistle split the shouts and limbs went limp.
You put awa your grizzly,
tied a loose lace,
spat on the scuff and rubbed til it shone dully.

You telt me aboot it.
Gid tae ken it wis there, you said.
Ah went huntin mine,
a familiar tae get tae know.

Oor Moby: Möbius

Jane Goldman

(or swipe up from the bottom bezel)

GEO
SULLY
SUB
STANCE

GEO
SULLY
SUB
STANCE

      here her
      diamante

      scatters

      stop lights
      drops red

a green coign
a green coign
of vantage

           at vet
           corner

GEO
SULLY
SUB
STANCE

GEO
SULLY
SUB
STANCE

outside
    vivi
       secting

a room
    GEO
    SULLY
    SUB
    STANCE

    GEO
    SULLY
    SUB
    STANCE

who decided to archive the perimeter fence?

unhinge all the doors; swallow your key

on exit (in case of dry ice alarm)

try jawbone walk
at middle meadow
in light ruined moonlight
sans teeth sans jaw
without a whale

        or bring some knitting
        and a ball

    this is

    OOR MOBY
    OORURMOBY
    OORA'BODY'sMOBY
    MÖBIUS
    MOBYMÖBIUS
    MOBY(   )VET

    MOBYMERZ

MOBYDADA
MOBYMAMA
MOBYBECHET
MOBYBESSIE
MOBYMELLY
MOBYSTEIN
MOBYWOOLFENSTEIN
MOBYWEINSTEIN
MOBYWEST
MOBYMUIR
MOBYPULPY
MOBYAMPERSAND
MOBY&
MOBYPULPY&
MOBYSTAIN
MOBYFIN
MOBYFINFAROUT
MOBYFENÊTRE
MOBYWINDOWPEEL
MOBYSUGARDOCKS
MOBYHOWL
MOBYWRECK

MOBYVRBA

MOBYNINA
MOBYNANA
MOBYMODOTTI
MOBYPHALLE
MOBYPISSFACTORY
MOBYPIPPILOTTI
MOBY291
MOBY369
MOBYWEEREDBAR
MOBYOUTSIDE(THE NARRATIVE)
MOBYUNDIGEST
MOBYCU T

MOBYCCA
MOBYVERSEHEARSE
MOBYSUTTON
MOBY10RED

MOBYCAESURA
MOBYSPL
(MOBYTHRUFF)
MOBYSCREE
MOBYTENDER
MOBYGUTTER

MOBYMAYBE

MOBYGEO
MOBYGEOSULLY
MOBYGEOSULLYSUBSTANCE

MOBY
GEO
SULLY
SUB
STANCE

MOBYMÖBIUS

or:

1. Swipe up from the bottom bezel of your iPhone to bring up
   Control Center.

2. Tap the Flashlight button at the bottom left.

3. Point the LED flash on the back of your iPhone at whatever
   you want to light up.

Inner sound
Sound of Mull
Water Sound
(Excerpt from SUND)

Angela Rawlings

parentheses
shores
oars
ears

There was a storm here.
There was a glacier here.
There was a war here.
There was a family living
here. There was a death
here. Here, there was a
death. Here, there was a
family. Here, a war. A war
here. War here. Storm
here. There was a seminary
here. There was a submarine
here carrying twelve nuclear
        warheads with
        a launch range
        of 7,500 miles.

Bakkasund, Bangsund, Brandasund,
Brønnøysund, Burøysund, Egersund,
Eigersund, Eiksund, Farsund, Fjågesund,
Godøysund, Haugesund, Haugsjåsund,
Havøysund (Northern Sami: Ávanuorri),
Helgøysund, Herøysund, Hidrasund,
Hillesund, Hokksund, Hol i Tjeldsund,
Holmsund, Homborsund, Jåsund, Jøssund,
Jøssund, Kalvøysund, Kilsund, Knarrlagsund,
Kvalsund (Northern Sami: Ráhkkerávju),
Kvalsund, Krabbesund, Kristiansund,
Kroksund, Kvitsund, Langesund,
Lysøysundet, Mausund, Midsund,
Minnesund, Noresund, Norheimsund,
Ny Hellesund, Nyksund, Ramsund,
Randesund, Rugsund, Sagasund,
Skjernøysund, Stamsund, Stokksund,
Sund, Sund, Sund, Sund i Lofoten,
Sundal, Sundbyfoss, Sunde, Sunde i Matre,
Sunde i Sunnhordland, Sundebru, Sundene,
Sundlia, Sundnes, Sundsbø, Sundve, Sundvollen,
Sundøya, Svinesund, Trongsundet, Tveitsund,
Ulvøysund, Vallersund, Vennesund,
Vikersund, Ålesund, Årøysund

Polaroids of Haemorrhoids

Stephen Watt

Consider your definition of art.

Fur coats stitched to the back of chairs,
      dragons made from drainpipes,
inflatable dolls shagging in pairs,
      the myth-science study of stereotypes,

a chair devoid of legs,
      a pair of broken aeroplane wings,
used condoms lying on an unmade bed,
      an operatic choir which sings,

a small calf bisected
      floating inside a turquoise tank,
Hitchcock's Psycho redirected
      like some churlish student prank,

iron figures bent at ninety degree angles,
      lightbulbs that switch on – and then off
(Wouldn't it be simpler to just burn some candles
      placed inside a bottle of Smirnoff?)

A shrine of mirrors,
      a stepladder upholstered in velvet,
a dozen laundry machines turned into cameras,
      fragments of items which have been bulleted,

81 cassette tapes filled with recorded rural sounds,
      three-dimensional garden sheds pulled apart,
the House of Osama Bin Laden (not cave nor underground)
      then where do you even start

considering my designs, my schemes,
      my purpose when unemployed,
to capture on film the swollen veins
      of my Turner Prize-winning haemorrhoids.

See that fossil? That's your mum, that is.

The Entirely Accurate Encyclopedia of Evolution
Robert Newman

Freight Books, RRP £11.99, 167pp

Rob Newman has written several novels but is still probably best known for his political and scientifically-minded stand-up comedy. His recent show *The New Theory of Evolution* has mutated into this book, a hybrid of scientific information and comedy about evolutionary biology; its raison-d'etre to criticise what Newman calls the 'dog-eat-dog' selfish gene version of evolution as popularised by Richard Dawkins.

Dawkin's theory states the gene is the most important aspect of an organism, and measures its success solely in terms of replicability in future generations, rendering any apparent cooperative or altruistic behaviour in its host organism an illusion. Newman, however, believes this narrow view of evolution has led to disastrous consequences for our understanding of society and behaviour. If, for example, we can explain human violence by the 'fact' that this is simply the cost of having genes that aren't bothered about their effect on other organisms, then there is little point in trying to change this essential aspect of ourselves. A recurring target for Newman's criticism is language – in particular that problematic adjective 'selfish'. Dawkins consistently claims gross misuse of his term. He was

not *actually* saying that genes are driven by selfish motives, it was simply a metaphor. But a telling quote from Dawkins' work cited by Newman explains that "gene selfishness will usually give rise to selfishness in individual behaviour."'

Newman is not the first person to challenge Dawkins. Ever since *The Selfish Gene* was published in 1974, other biologists and philosophers have been queuing up to point out the apparent errors in both the logic and the evidence. Dawkins' representation of what a gene is – analogous to a bit of information that operates completely independently of other genes, the host organism's wider genome and the environment – is quite dated. We now know these interactions are crucial to the way that each gene expresses itself, and this new field of 'epigenetics' offers a much richer and more nuanced understanding of evolution.

The *Encyclopaedia* itself is not a linear argument but rather a series of entries about different pieces of research that summarise evidence against Dawkins' work. To get his points across, Newman tells some very funny stories. My favourite is about a spider who makes replicas of herself out of chewed-up insect husks, and nobody knows why. It seems to be a successful survival strategy, but Newman points out that we cannot attribute selfish motives to this behaviour; perhaps she's just lonely.

Does Newman succeed? Partly. There is not enough detail either about the theory of evolution itself nor about Dawkins' book to be able to fully understand Newman's counter-argument. And there is little point in simply summarising observations of altruistic behaviours as evidence against Dawkins, when *The Selfish Gene* specifically sets out to explain altruism. But the book does well at conveying the fact that genetics is not a finished project, it's very much a work in progress – an important point to balance against how the subject (and much of science) is often taught.

It's a fun, lively read, and Newman is at his comedic best when angrily ripping into some of the worst cases of Dawkinsitis. And why shouldn't science be communicated through comedy? Anything that breaks down the barrier around such difficult and complex subject matter deserves to be applauded.

– Bear of little brain

Future Tense

Lie of the Land
Michael F Russell

Polygon, £12.99, 304pp

Given the state of the country at the moment, it's perhaps unsurprising that dystopian science fiction is enjoying something of a revival. With Dan Grace's *Winter* and David Mitchell's *The Bone Clocks* showing Scotland and Ireland respectively collapsing in on themselves, Michael F Russell's *Lie of the Land* is a welcome and terrifying addition to the conversation.

When Carl, a journalist living in Glasgow under Fascistic state control, receives information and a sample of some new piece of technology, he heads

to Inverlair in pursuit of a big scoop. While there SCOPE, a new private sector communications web, is turned on and, whether through design or accident, the resonance causes nationwide pain, nose bleeds and death. Trapped in the village, a 'notspot', a hole in coverage, Carl struggles to settle in a place that may have saved his life but which feels more like a prison camp than a haven. In many ways it's a classic set up: the reader travels with an outsider into a community and watches as the new dynamic ruptures already fragile relationships.

What follows is a gripping story of rural infighting and bare survivalism. The residents of Inverlair can only assume that everyone else in the country is dead. Loved ones who were away from the village won't be coming back. It all gets a bit *Lord of the Flies* when the stronger men band together and rig the rationing system to favour themselves and use violence to get their way. A cast of misfits including drug-growing Terry, home-brew making Hendrik, a group of teenagers who play chicken with the deadly waves encircling the village as a way to break the monotony, and Alec the 'stalker', a lonely figure responsible for hunting deer and keeping the village in meat, enliven what could be a depressing scenario.

It's rural noir in a near-future setting, all the more terrifying for how plausible each speculation is.

One of 'post-event' science fiction's problems is that the most dramatic moment in the story – the 'event' that causes the breakdown of society – necessarily comes at the beginning. To combat this, Russell uses an interesting structure, moving back and forth in time to heighten tension and create an air of mystery about what exactly happened in the immediate aftermath of SCOPE being turned on. It is also to his credit that he shows and explains the event, rather than taking the all too common easy way out by having some non-specific catastrophe semi-forgotten in the mists of time. By extrapolating from current technology, science and political trends, Russell has sculpted an end of the world that seems not only plausible, but potentially imminent.

It's heartening to see this book brought out by a publisher like Polygon and marketed without all the usual trappings, winks and apologies that science fiction often receives from 'mainstream' publishing. With writers like Michel Faber recently returning to science fiction, David Mitchell diving into deep fantasy waters and Kazuo Ishiguro writing about a thoroughly real and unallegorical dragon, the 'M Barrier' as I call it (named for the M inserted in Iain Banks's name to distinguish between 'genre' and 'mainstream' works) is finally breaking down. I hope Polygon will continue to support writing like this.

– *Totoro*

Gothic Gravitational Pull

On the Edges of Vision
Helen McClory

Queens Ferry Press, £9.99, 174pp

In 2015, Helen McClory's *On The Edges of Vision* beat many excellent homegrown books published last year to win the Saltire Society Scottish First Book of the Year. It's a feat not only remarkable in that the book's small independent publisher Queen's Ferry Press hails from Texas, USA, but also that it's a collection of short stories, too often disqualified from entry to debut writing awards. The title of McClory's first publication, then, is curiously fitting for an outsider. The Saltire Society's recognition of this book has validated a new writing talent that may otherwise have gone unnoticed and uncelebrated by larger, London-based book awards (and the accompanying national press fanfare) whose limiting criteria may exclude literary joys from small independent publishers willing to take a gamble on their convictions with short stories, or works are more varied in their origin.

McClory's author bio states "There is a moor and a cold sea in her heart," a whimsy that succinctly encapsulates the collection's poignant, gravitational pull towards the gothic. The stories within the pleasingly, deceptively sunny yellow cover emerge as if from Pandora's Box: tipping open the ordinarily lurking, surreal gristliness of life into where things grow weird around the boundaries.

Free from the debut trope of self-reference and loosely-disguised autobiography, McClory engages in a kind of inquisitive modern mythmaking. Within settings as diverse as forests, airports and ideal homes, a pleasing jumble of styles and references emerge: fantasy, horror, classicism, fairytales, and other dark flavours. Such macabre turns bring to mind the terror of Ann Radcliffe or poetic justice of Roald Dahl. One flesh-eating picnic scene, in particular, evokes Dahl's 'Lamb to the Slaughter', but moreishly fresh in its own sense.

Occasionally, McClory attacks idealised versions of domesticity and commercialism, painting uncanny blooms that she studs with thorns of knowing social commentary. A thirteen year old girl listens to a mixtape named "Misandry and Pink Glitter" and doesn't know what it means but thinks it sounds "cool". The delightfully named "Tablescapes!" sees the taping of a festive cooking TV show descend into surreal hysteria worthy of the title's exclamation mark. 'Pecan Pie', a seductive highlight, is set in an all-night diner as two strangers meet and interact, testing limits: "Whatever he'll do next she'll do right back." It's a heady study of light and shade, voluptuous sexual tension, ambiguous danger and gender tropes that, deliciously, has a lot in common with film noir.

Whilst the stories do, towards the end, fall into a pattern that anticipates supernatural elements will appear from where there are none at first sight, this is a slight weakness and not enough to diminish the strength of the individual stories. These tales are on the short side of the short story and fit their form well; making it an accomplished and vivid collection of compact storytelling, and a debut worthy of its award. I started reading late one night and continued long into the strange AM, glad of the accidental perfect timing. Life is weird, if you know where to look. McClory knows where to look—and how to write about it.

– *Laura Waddell*

Bathymetry of the soul

The Outrun
Amy Liptrot

Canongate, RRP £14.99, 280 pp

Early in Amy Liptrot's sparkling memoir, on one of her frequent midnight haven't-drunk enough-to-sleep cycle rides through deserted London chasing 'the sensation of escape', she swerves out of control, toppling off a towpath into a canal. This self-destructive accident is no outlier: she's lived dangerously and desperately, a fish out of water among partying, nightclub-loving mates, whose company she leaves early to drink more quickly alone. Later, a few hard-won sober months on, after losing friends, jobs, flats and her partner, she returns to what was her parents' farm on Orkney, back to where she was born and grew up, but never seemed to belong. Fearing it's possible she may drink again, she ponders whether a 'small, careful life' here could hold her.

She aches for her ex, can't imagine how to dance sober and describes poignantly the moment she discovers renouncing drink doesn't mean her sex life is over. Yet she demonstrates immense fearlessness and strength in remaining mostly alone, working nights tracking corncrakes for the RSPB, traveling "to where the internet ends". Here she constantly searches and researches (perhaps addictively, she concedes) on land and online, to find out all she can about everything she sets eyes on: geology, clouds, shipwrecks, seals. Visiting the uninhabited island the Holm of Papay, she contemplates asking to be left to spend the night in a chambered tomb. "I crave either life in the inner city or to go to islands beyond islands, islands of the dead."

She is passionately curious – about marine traffic, flight radar and, of course, herself, her childhood, her parents' divorce, her addiction. She swims in ice cold water, addicted to how it jolts her system, and prompts thoughts of the ECT her father underwent for bipolar disorder. She adjusts to the slow rhythms of drystone dyking, carefully building, lifting heavy coping stones to bind the two sides of wall. She records storms and gales, greylag geese and breaking waves, uploading the sounds to the internet where her London friends can listen to her life.

In the brilliant chapter 'Online', she notes how technology tracks sharks and seabirds, measures ocean depths, records every song she listens to, plots her daily activities and movements, sleep and menstrual cycles – locates her. "I am not tracking a mysterious or endangered species," she says, "I am carrying out semi-scientific studies into myself, performing bathymetry of the soul."

Her achievement, if she can hold on to it, seems to be in turning simultaneously from and towards life on the edge. She says, of the elements, "I want to see if these forces will weigh me down, like coping stones, and stop the jolting."

Praised by, among others, Jenni Fagan, Will Self and Stuart Kelly, this is a beautiful, intelligent, meditative debut, offering magical depths through a study of fierce vulnerability.

–Jabberwocky

A Light That Never Goes Out

The Waves Burn Bright
Iain Maloney

Freight Books, RRP £9.99, 277 pp

Iain Maloney risks strong reaction to his latest novel *The Waves Burn Bright,* which has 1988's Piper Alpha North Sea oil platform disaster as its major event. Writing about real life in fiction is fraught with danger, but when your book concerns a notorious catastrophe, research and point of view is vital if you are not to be accused of disrespect or worse. You not only have to be sure of yourself and how you're going to approach it, you must do so with conviction. Even then you have to be prepared for unfounded opprobrium, such as James Robertson with his 2013 novel *The Professor of Truth*; not towards the book itself, but simply the writing of it.

Maloney's awareness of the duty of care he has to all involved shows in his writing, which is never sensationalist and backed by rigorous research, as he takes on more than one controversial and emotive subject. One of his central characters, Marcus Fraser, suffers survivor's guilt and PTSD as a result of his involvement on Piper Alpha, and his alcoholism could be seen as a form of self-medication. But it's not as simple as that; it's never as simple as that. Problem drinking, while common in Scottish writing, has rarely been dealt with in such an evenhanded and non-reactionary manner. In fact, the way Maloney deals with all of these topics speaks of a writer who can not only understand and empathise with others, but who urges his readers do likewise.

Having read previous work by Maloney I would suggest *The Waves Burn Bright* sees an assured step forward in his writing in terms of people and place. His depiction of Aberdeen in particular will ring true with anyone who knows the city. Details of pubs, cafes and back streets are written with the confidence of someone who knows them like the back of his hand, and Maloney also manages to convey that city's individuality, something which has been affected by the discovery of oil in general, and Piper Alpha specifically. Likewise, Korea, Japan and Hawaii are portrayed with equal credibility as Maloney's other central character, Marcus's daughter Carrie Fraser, traverses the globe to try and discover who she is, and to avoid discovering who her father has become.

The secondary characters make less of an impact, although I have a particular fondness for Hannah, Carrie's mother, whose lack of sympathy and empathy for a hurt child will chime strongly with anyone brought up in a family with a medical practitioner. However, this is understandable. It's rare to have one memorable character in a novel, but with the disparate double act of this estranged father and daughter Maloney has created two, each as flawed and single-minded as the other. You don't just want to know what happens to them, you care.

The Waves Burn Bright is Iain Maloney's best book to date, not only an entertaining and thoughtful one, but, I would suggest, an important one. Many of us will never forget the night of Piper Alpha, but there will be many who are unaware of it. This is an important part of Scotland's history and Maloney not only pays respect to the memory of that terrible event, he offers fresh insight into how individuals and their families and friends cope – or more often fail to cope – with trauma, and the humanity behind the headlines.

– *Kes*

Monster Mash

The Wolf Trial
Neil Mackay

Freight Books, RRP £13.99, 375pp

In 16th century Germany Peter Stumpf is put on trial for a killing spree so horrific his superstitious town of Bideburg wants to execute him as a werewolf. Enter war-veteran turned lawyer Paulus Melchior, the hard-headed rationalist determined to prove Stumpf is merely human, albeit monstrous, and in so doing save Stumpf's family from torture and a sinful death. Into this bubbling cauldron, Neil Mackay throws a light seasoning of the supernatural, but is this genre horror he's concocting or something darker?

Monsters are, after all, no longer scary: we've turned vampires into sex symbols, zombies into a laughing stock, and elf kings get fabulous hair. Yet all these fiends make surprisingly chilling cameos on account of Mackay's unflinching description of their all-too-human origins: toxic superstition and a fear of science. It's one hell of an accomplishment.

Here, the real monster is man. More monstrous, however, are the self-inflicted cataclysms of the Black Death, the Peasants' revolt and the disastrous Munster Rebellion, which serve as the historical and psychological backdrop to *The Wolf Trial's* feature creature. These characters know horror real enough to shake anyone's faith in God, or kick it into psychopathic mania. One early aside tells of Paulus' visit to a village so shaken by the plague they'll try anything to stay sane, including paganism. His priestly friend Carolus Fromme burns them all, killing more in one day than the werewolf he's so keen to skin alive, and feels no guilt. Deeper in the forest, children go "frogging" – an act of animal cruelty that in Mackay's hands speaks more of the sadism at the core of man's heart than any number of flambéed witches.

In fact, once you've made it out the other side, it's possible to look back on this nightmarish tale and view the *The Wolf Trial's* supernatural elements as cynical window dressing, a gingerbread house designed to entice readers seeking fantastical escapism into a torture chamber of historical truths. Mackay even has Willie Loos, our narrator and Paulus' assistant, justify the distinction:

"[have] in my make-up a love of stories which make sense of the past, not fairy tales concocted by rich poets who have the resources to spend all day lying on their couch dreaming up fantasies that the world does not need."

What we need, Mackay seems to suggest, is some big-picture honesty. In this world there are child soldiers and murderous bigots, rapists and paedophiles, blood thirst and blind service and unfathomable stupidity, but no monsters – only people, as fallible and broken and easily led in the 16th century as they are today.

Given such unwavering and forthright dissection of the human condition, it feels churlish to fault Mackay for anything, but if the novel stumbles it does so only in the finer details of construction. The history of Bideburg, Paulus' memories of Munster and other characters' backstories are delivered through monologues that flirt with a world-building blasphemy: the infodump. While gripping and essential, these chapter-long asides increasingly slow the narration to an undead shamble, even though you feel the story wants to dart through the woods with a breakneck lupine grace.

Part historical fiction, part supernatural gorefest, part legal drama, *The Wolf Trial* is a strange beast, sutured together with stitches showing for affect. Its representation of mankind at its worst is at once mesmerising, honest and horrific. It shouldn't work, it should fall apart at the seams, but Neil Mackay's electric prose gives his creation a blast of effortless, truly terrifying life.

– Dangerous Beans

Dinosaurs

Dialogue On the Dark
Nuala Watt

Calder Wood Press, RRP £5, 28pp

For those of us who watched *Jurassic Park* at nine years old, Sam Neill's advice was nothing less than survival strategy: if – and when – you are someday confronted by a tyrannosaurus, do not move. The fact the monsters could only see moving objects was left to one side, and I'd never paused to consider what their world must have looked like until reading Nuala Watt's 'The Eye Chart'. The poem, along with several others in *Dialogue On the Dark*, takes as its starting point Watt's experiences as a

partially-sighted person and, had a more enlightened scientist attempted to test the limits of *T. rex's* vision, they might too have found it encountering her "alphabets / as small as atoms" and "letters ... illegible as stars".

Her collection begins with a riposte against John Milton, whose standing and waiting are defied by Watt's updated assertions: "I eat, sleep, kiss, swear, get children dressed. / I feel and write." Throughout its twenty-two poems there is a compelling theme of bringing the ancient up to date with the modern. The powerfully damning 'Scold's Bridle' connects the silencing effects of shaming and catcalling to the titular medieval torture device used to physically render women incapable of speaking. Its flipside is found in 'The Ain Sakhri Lovers', which takes as its subject a less chaste piece of statuary than the Arundel tomb, considering its carver's motivations in depicting "The first lust in art". Though what survives of them is sex, Watt also finds in their eternal coupling a hope that "through four retinas, life might seem clear".

Though no actual dinosaurs (apart from Milton) appear, Watt's world is nevertheless populated by a bestiary of other fantastic creatures, beginning with 'Floors', in which a snakelike woman feels her way across "the river-cool floor / of the Doomsday Book house / unsettling old women", and continuing through the mythical pairing of 'Mermaid' and 'Selkie', which cleverly depict the casual shock of their two subjects being discovered in the present day. And, perhaps unsurprisingly, there is the woman who, in 'Map', navigates a set of busy city streets by echolocation, letting "her voice bounce / back to shocked ears". By its end, her metamorphic decision is made with the certainty which marks almost all of Watt's subject matter: "she'll join the bat clan".

Hers is a poetry without fear of the unknown or any hedging of bets; its images are sharp, carrying the sense they have been long in their honing, the embodiment of Watt's stated goal "to make a sense I'm neither banned nor blessed / but breathing here". Her gaze burns through the subtitles of the foreign film in 'Pictures', grasping at the argument between its characters as if hearing them through tenement walls. Sitting in the cinema, I covered my eyes as Lex and Tim were chased around a stainless-steel maze; squinting at blurry velociraptors, they lost their form and threat as my imagination imposed itself upon the action. In 'Watching Kathak', Watt makes out dancers as "a swarm of bees / Another is grey light", whilst "drummers lose their legs. / Half torso, half music". As she sways in her chair, watching and listening, her words admit a further possibility: that what one cannot see, one might become.

–Ruski

Memories and Myths

Kitsune
Jane McKie

Cinnamon Press, RRP £8.99, 80pp

Reading a poetry collection is like going to a party. You don't expect to like everyone you meet, but if you're lucky there are some good conversations to be enjoyed, and some memorable people. Occasionally, one encounter will really stand out and make a lasting impression. Reading *Kitsune* makes one such lasting impression. A single poem, 'Rannoch', made the whole book worthwhile:

"A wilderness peopled by ifrits:
    The first a hinny, horse-headed-mule-legged, running
        with a sideways gait
        against the wind. She brays.
Stops.

    Brays.   Stops."

This is assured, utterly vivid writing. We don't need to be told what an *ifrit* is, as we can deduce that it's some kind of being-of-fire. In fact it's a middle-eastern fire spirit, one of many far-flung creatures of myth that Jane McKie brings to bear on familiar things. Here the light on the lochan, the rowan tree in berries and autumn grass all blaze right through the poem to the last, smoking peat hag line. One can never look at the moor the same way again. This collection of poems from the immensely accomplished Edinburgh-based poet Jane McKie is lavishly spiced with memories and myths. The title, *Kitsune*, is the Japanese word for fox, which is traditionally believed to have magical powers, particularly the ability to shape-shift into a man or woman. In the title poem the fox is a lover, contemplating her need to wear her human form as "a veil or shell... because it is my mask you love." Throughout the collection there is a sense of a hidden self hiding within the outer display, as if the real writer of the poems lives life in perpetual disguise. She uses myths and legends in intriguing ways, like a child with a dressing-up box.

Motherhood is a strong theme in the collection, working particularly well with the portrayal of mythical mothers, such as that of the Monster of Ravenna. In 'The Ocean Describes Montauk Point', the relationship between the sea and rock has all the complex rhythms of the love between mother and child, wife and husband or daughter and father: "I want it, only to lose my hunger. / Resent it, only to drown my anger... I relish its nearness/then run a mile."

As well as myth, the collection makes good use of memory: grits around which bright pearls form. In 'Lake above the clouds', a series of fourteen, sometimes startling, images present a long, high-altitude solo walk. Here nature is a cleansing, redemptive force. "A cloud of butterflies, / wings freckled with peppercorns. / They staple themselves to my hands and face / to feed off the salt." In some poems it is as if only memory matters. In 'The specious present', "clock hands tremble on the same damn minute", as if the here and now cannot

be trusted. In 'The Wind in the Mountains', "fulfilment lies in leaving..." the experience of a hill climb, as this is when it will become memory.

A feature of Jane McKie's style is an ambiguous use of 'we', and 'you', which sometimes seems to include us, the readers, but other times not. 'Perhaps we might start now' (the opening poem) begins, "Perhaps we might be kind to each other / all the time." It soon becomes unclear whether we are all being asked to show more compassion for all living creatures or whether this is a private conversation between the poet and her lover. Are we in on the secret, or eavesdropping? Are we seeing the poet's true self, or just another disguise? Sometimes maddening, often intriguing, this is a masked ball of a party.

–Spectacled Bear

Nature Poetry and the Art of Surprise

The Weight of Light
Chris Powici

Red Squirrel Publishing, RRP £8.99, 63 pp

Of all the poetic genres, it seems that writers of nature poetry struggle hardest to follow Ezra Pound's advice to "make it new". A stag on a highland crag has looked exactly the same for a very long time. This symbolic image is a well-mined topic, along with daffodils moving in the breeze and bramble-picking. Nature poetry is so ubiquitous that it has become difficult for a writer to invoke the profound emotional response that is one of poetry's enduring pleasures. There have been many attempts to find a new direction for nature poetry in the 21ˢᵗ century. Greg Wren argued in the *American Poetry Review* that contemporary nature poetry should address environmental problems. At one extreme this leads to worthy rhetoric, at the other the impenetrable postmodernism of Peter Larkin in *Give Forest Its Next Portent*.

Powici "makes it new" by reaching within himself, metaphorically pulling a rabbit out of his heart and changing the way we see the world. He achieves this magic trick by harnessing the unconscious as well as the intellect. Thomas Tranströmer, one of Powici's major influences, is a master of the sudden change in perspective and his work yields a particularly clear example. In the 'The Couple', the bedside lamp is switched off and "its white shade / glimmers for a moment before dissolving / like a tablet in a glass of darkness". Those last words suddenly widen our perspective; darkness, with all the word's undertones and associations, is given agency, the ability to dissolve light. Powici does something similar in 'The Deer'. The first three stanzas make skilful use of anapaests to simulate the sound and movement of deer, then he uses an image which stops us in our tracks: "snow is the dust / of the bones of deer / falling to earth". The perspective widens to include countless generations of deer, the earth's natural cycle of life and death. In 'Geoff', the eponymous figure is feeding garden birds when a blue tit "flutters to the shed roof / and beats the snowflakes from its wings / until it's more

blizzard than bird". This time Powici evokes a startlingly vivid image, focussing on detail rather than changing the perspective.

The lines often have the spiritual resonance of haiku. During an interview with Andrew F. Giles in *New Linear Perspectives*, Powici says "there's an element of the religious/spiritual about how I think and feel about nature". This veneration, often implicit, becomes explicit in 'Otter Goddess' and in the last line of 'The Hare' when he describes its "god-eyed stare". There are strong descriptions of epiphanic experiences scattered throughout this book.

The title of the collection is taken from a fine two-line poem, entitled 'Oak': "these hundred thousand sun-hammered leaves / this weight of light". This phrase has been borrowed from physics. It refers to the fact that photons have no mass but are affected by gravity so, in a sense, have weight. In 'Snows', Powici fails to appreciate the "miracle or holy" in the nuclear world: a world he cannot see. He floats in the shallows of quantum physics, mentioning but not really engaging with his muons and neutrinos. Some of these references work reasonably well but the use of 'quantumly' in the prose poem, 'All The Time Billions', feels uncharacteristically clumsy.

Interspersed in this collection are a number of touching family poems addressing loss. It is significant that these poems describe shared experiences out-of-doors; picnics, gardening and fishing. This is felicitous as it is Powici's descriptions of the natural world which shine the brightest. As long as the reader is not misled by the title into expecting a deeper appreciation and exploration of science they will be enchanted by seeing nature through Powici's reverential eyes.

–Kanga Kangeroo

A Sing o a Scotland

Tonguit
Harry Giles

Freight Books £8.99, 72pp

> "We have to get to the root of the problem.
> We need to be clear where the origin of love lie.
> And we should be clear what we mean by this term.
> It is apolitical ideology supported by minorities…"

In 'Sermon' from his first collection *Tonguit* Harry Giles adapts a speech given by David Cameron to the Munich Security Conference on 5 February 2011 by replacing the words 'terrrorism', 'security', and 'Islamic extremism' with the word 'love'. To insert the same word repeatedly into a pre-existing text might seem like a fairly minor poetic action. However I think the resulting poem showcases a key strength of this collection: its political force.

One would expect a sermon to exhort its listeners towards, rather than away from, love. However, the poem says 'we should cut ourselves off from love', here presented as a seditious element that is eroding a collective identity. In this, Giles highlights the erosion of compassion that is necessary to sustain the inequality that current government policies exacerbate. 'Sermon' performs a growing compassion deficit in British politics through a simple but profound poetic choice. Despite my own personal bias against found poems, this example shows the genre at its best.

'Sermon' is preceded by 'Your Strengths', another found poem that combines questions from the Department of Work and Pensions Work Capability Assessment, the Life In The UK Citizenship Test and the eponymous psychometric test, also used by the DWP. Giles makes skilful use of juxtaposition and much of this poem is almost farcical. It is unclear how knowing who defeated the Vikings increases your value as a British citizen, or the following:

> "Can you put on a hat?
> Can you turn on a tap?
> Who is the patron saint of Scotland?"

The barrage of possibly inappropriate questions on everything from police procedure to bowel function makes the poem increasingly claustrophobic. It creates two forms of hysteria: wild laughter and mounting panic. One of the few good things I can say about the current government is that it provokes excellent satire, which Giles utilises well.

These two poems, constructed using material already in the public domain, explore the fabricated and subjective nature of modern British identity. Poems in Scots critique the local variety.

> "A sing o a Scotland which hasna gied tae Skye
> or Scrabster

or Scone
   bit cin do ye an absolute
      dymont o
a rant on the plurality o
    Scots
identity, fae Alexandair mac
Alexandair tae Wee Eck."

The Scots used in *Tonguit* is a mixture of many dialects – the notes call it "mongrel and magpie... with a few personal variations". Is it presented as a quasi-universal Scots? It can be dense and forbidding on the page:

"A beam british agin yer
American orthodoxy, faimlie:
ye're hella glaise n thay greens
gust puir bangin tae a tannin tongue
but A rackon A greet ironic, grin
mair weblike as gridplan.
           (Reception.)"

The poem may work better in performance where tone of voice and body language provide information not available in print.

However, in spite of these reservations it is clear to me that Giles is writing himself into the Scottish tradition. 'Brave' suggests influences including Edwin Morgan's urban poems and Hugh MacDiarmid's *A Drunk Man Looks At The Thistle*. The phrase "I sing" echoes George Mackay Brown's phrase 'for the islands I sing', perhaps to announce another excellent Orcadian poet. Significantly, 'I sing' is also the first verb of Virgil's *Aeneid* – epic poets sing. Giles promises to be a politically vibrant presence in Scottish poetry for a long time to come.

– *The Dormouse*

Dear Gutter

After a year apart I've been reunited with my partner but our teenage daughter has rejected me.

After 18 years together, half of which was tough going, my partner and I decided to split. After a year apart and having both seen other people, we realised the depth of our love and started dating again. We'd always kept a lid on our problems so the split came as a total shock to our daughter, who was fourteen at the time. We didn't tell her we were seeing each other again straight away, partly to see how things went between us and partly because she had crucial exams approaching. We didn't want to destabilise her life at such an important time. Now the exams are out of the way, her mother has broken the news and my daughter is deeply upset. Most difficult for me is that her ire is directed at me alone, which is heart-breaking. I have no plans to move back in till she leaves home, but how do I go about rebuilding a relationship with a daughter I love heart and soul?

Gutter says

Being sixteen can be the most difficult age in one's whole life. It's a point at which the tectonic plates of childhood and adulthood rub hard. The teenager strives for independence of body and mind, trying out new experiences and opinions, but can lack the emotional library through which adults gain perspective.

By the sounds of it, you and your partner have been smart in waiting to break the news. Clearly the original split was traumatic for all three of you. It's likely that, after you left the family home, your partner's understandable anger was tangible, whether overtly or more subtly, and that your daughter picked up on this. Whoever departed, your daughter was going to feel both protective of the parent who stayed behind and very rejected herself, regardless of the circumstances.

In handling the rejection you're experiencing which, coming from your own child must hurt a great deal (and no doubt seems unfair when in all probability degrees of blame lie with both you and your partner) remember that it comes from your daughter's own feelings of abandonment and betrayal. Hard though it might be, it's vital to not meet rejection with further defensive rejection, as this will open an ever-widening fissure between the two of you.

After the rapprochement, rather than being happy for her parents as one might imagine, your daughter may well be reconnecting with the very difficult emotions associated with her experience of the break-up, feelings that have become inextricably linked to her memory of the time her parents were still together. You'll know yourself how, many years later, one or two negative memories from childhood can cast a pall over our perception of the past, obscuring years of stability and happiness.

As far as your daughter's concerned, her parents' relationship may now be associated with danger. She's had none of the emotional benefits of the rekindling of romance so may see it as a threat. Despite her outward teenage bravado, at such a young age she'll be feeling very vulnerable and will lack the skills to unpick the tangle of feelings.

Therefore, in order to build bridges, you'll have to both acknowledge your own sense of rejection (let's face it, ignoring it won't work) while also seeing things squarely from your daughter's point-of-view. While teenagers hate it when their parents lay an emotional burden on them, if you get a chance to talk about any of what has happened, then seize it, but treading carefully as you go. However, that opportunity may never arise. If that is the case, most important thing is to reiterate your unconditional love in both word and deed.

The good news is that we all mellow. As she gets older, leaves home and builds new relationships of her own, you may be surprised at how quickly she softens. As the saying goes, 'At sixteen I discovered my father was an idiot. At twenty-one I was amazed at how much he'd learned in five years'.

It's also worth remembering that it's very healthy to realise, as a teenager, that your Dad's an arse. Although it may not feel like it at the moment, your daughter's rejection may well be a positive expression of her developing independence and a very normal experience for parents up and down the country. Fate has decreed that you're the one who gets it in the neck but over time her anger will most likely dissipate.

If you have a problem you'd like advice on send it to deargutter@gmail.com

Contributor Biographies

Laura R. Becherer is a doctoral student in creative writing at the University of Glasgow. She writes fiction and poetry.

Tessa Berring is an Edinburgh based artist. Poetry publications include journals *Nutshells and Nuggets*, *Magma*, and *Leopard skin and Limes*.

Andrew Blair is that straight white poet with the beard.

William Bonar was shortlisted in 2015 for a New Writers Award. His award winning pamphlet, *Offering*, is available at www.redsqirrelpress.com

Alistair Braidwood runs the Scottish cultural website Scots Whay Hae! and his reviews are found in the more discerning publications.

Mark Buckland is a former publisher who now works in television.

Ian Burgham is author of six collections of poetry. His latest work, *Midnight*, was launched in 2015.

R.A. Davis was born in Edinburgh in 1983. He grew up in Kent and North Wales and belongs to Glasgow.

Brian Docherty lives in East Sussex. He has published 4 books, including *Independence Day*, (Penniless Press, 2015).

Leonie Dunlop is a writer and toponymist. She has recently handed in her PhD and is looking forward to new ventures.

Jim Ferguson is a poet and prose writer based in Glasgow. Jim has been writing and publishing since 1986 and is presently a Creative Writing Tutor at Glasgow Kelvin College in Glasgow's East End.

Alec Finlay (1966–) poet and artist, has published over thirty books. Blogs at alecfinlay.com

Paul Foy has had short stories published in various publications. He works as a freelance filmmaker and educator.

Jane Goldman is Reader in English at Glasgow University. *Border Thoughts* (Leamington Books, 2014) is her first slim volume.

Pippa Goldschmidt is an Edinburgh-based writer of fiction, poems and non-fiction. She's a winner of the 2016 Suffrage Science award (for women in science).

Catherine Graham is author of five acclaimed poetry collections. Her most recent collection, *Her Red Hair Rises with the Wings of Insects*, was a finalist for various awards. www.catherinegraham.com

Mandy Haggith is a writer and environmental activist. Her most recent novel is *Bear Witness*.

Steven Heighton is a poet, fiction writer, and reviewer for the *New York Times Book Review*. His latest books are *The Waking Comes Late* (poetry), *The Dead Are More Visible* (stories), and *Workbook* (essays).

Andy Jackson's collection *A Beginner's Guide to Cheating* is out now on Red Squirrel Press. He is also co-editor of the *Scotia Extremis* project at scotiaextremis. wordpress.com

Marc David Jacobs is a freelance writer and arts worker. In 2016, he released an album called *Songs for Thistlists*.

Auður Jónsdóttir is an Icelandic author, playwright and freelance journalist. Her latest novel, *Gran Mal* (Stóri skjálfti), was published in Reykjavík and is Audur's most successful novel to date.

Russell Jones is an Edinburgh-based writer and editor. His recent full poetry collection was published by Freight Books.

James Kelman is a Booker Prize winning novelist. His latest book *Dirt Road* is published by Canongate.

Catriona Knapman is a Scottish writer and development worker. Read more about her writing and performances: facebook.com/luckydiplife.

Gerry Loose is a poet whose works include books and off-page installations in galleries, Botanic Gardens and other landscapes.

Jeanette Lynes's seventh collection of poetry, *Bedlam Cowslip: The John Clare Poems* was shortlisted for two Saskatchewan Book Awards. She is also the author of a novel, *The Factory Voice*. She directs the MFA in Writing at the University of Saskatchewan, Canada.

Rob A. Mackenzie's most recent collection is *The Good News* (Salt, 2013). He is from Glasgow and lives in Leith.

SR Mackison a Persian who migrated to Britain four years ago. This story reflects my real life experience as a refugee.

Marianne MacRae is a Creative Writing PhD candidate at the University of Edinburgh, studying talking animals in poetry.

Iain Maloney is the author of three novels, *First Time Solo*, *Silma Hill* and *The Waves Burn Bright*. @iainmaloney

Mikhail Mavrotheris was born in Nicosia. He's an ok kiddo, and is wandering somewhere: mentally + physically. Believe him, yes?

Ellen McAteer is a Clydebuilt poet and songwriter. She founded Tell It Slant poetry bookshop and lecturers at the Glasgow School of Art.

Andrew McCallum lives and works in the Scottish Southlands. He's a big fan of Nordic noir and symphonic metal.

James McGonigal's latest collection is The Camphill Wren (Red Squirrel Press, 2016).

Helen McClory won the Saltire First Book of the Year Award 2015 with her debut collection *On the Edges of Vision*.

Carol McKay writes fiction, life writing and poetry, and teaches creative writing through The Open University. carolmckay.co.uk

Kerrie McKinnel is a student on the University of Glasgow's MLitt Creative Writing. She is working on her first novel.

Rhona Millar lives in Glasgow. She has been featured in Litro, Quotation and Ink, Sweat and Tears amongst other publications.

Philip Miller is a journalist, poet and writer based in Edinburgh. His debut novel *The Blue Horse* came out in 2015, his second *All The Galaxies*, is to be published 2017.

Fiona Montgomery, a graduate of Glasgow University's Creative Writing MLitt, is a freelance journalist and is writing a memoir.

Iain Morrison has a collaborative writing habit. He recently threw a night of drag queen poetry at Scottish Poetry Library.

Christina Neuwirth was born in Austria and now lives in Edinburgh. Her novella *Amphibian* is currently shortlisted for the Novella Award. Contact: @gwynn255

Ignacio B. Peña is a full-time film animator who is now exploring a newly discovered passion for writing fiction.

Lauren Pope runs a summer school for creative writing and literature students at the University of Edinburgh.

A P Pullan was made in Yorkshire, and is now assigned to Ayrshire. My blog appi-jack.blogspot.co.uk is essential reading

Valgerður Þóroddsdóttir is founder and director of Partus, an independent publisher of poetry and prose based in Reykjavík.

Eveline Pye has an international reputation for statistical poetry. Her collection *Smoke That Thunders* was published in May 2015 by Mariscat.

Claire Quigley lives in Glasgow and works in digital technology education. Often found recklessly pressing the shutter button.

Angela Rawlings is an American-Canadian poet, librettist, editor, artist: whose genre-bending work embraces acoustic ecology, counter-mapping, improvisation, and ecopoetics.

Cynthia Rogerson is an award winning author, Program Director of the Moniack Mhor Writers Centre and Royal Literary Fellow.

Stewart Sanderson received an Eric Gregory Award in 2015. His first pamphlet is *Fios* (Tapsalteerie, 2015).

Hamish Scott is from Edinburgh. He has published three collections of his poetry in Scots with The Laverock's Nest Press.

Arun Sood is a writer and academic. He was born to an Indian father and West-Highland mother in Aberdeen, 1985.

Stobo: Alive: part two. Dad, astronomer, writer, trustee, sepsis survivor, time traveller and snowdancer extraordinaire. Aiming for a second Halley's Comet.

Malachy Tallack is a writer, editor and singer-songwriter from Shetland. His latest book, *The Un-discovered Islands*, is due out in October 2016.

Ryan Vance edits weird lit zine *The Queen's Head*, reads fiction for *The Island Review*, and likes your new haircut.

Paul Walton is an ornithologist living in Glasgow.

George T Watt writes almost exclusively in Scots, and why not!

Nuala Watt comes from Glasgow and has a PhD on the poetics of partial sight from the University of Glasgow.

Roseanne Watt is a writer/filmmaker from Shetland. She is poetry editor for the online literary magazine *The Island Review*.

Stephen Watt, author of 'Spit' and 'Optograms', is a Dumbarton punk poet who reviews for The Mumble + Louder Than War.

Christie Williamson is from Yell in Shetland and lives in Glasgow. His latest publication is *Oo an Feddirs* (Luath).

Ross Wilson lives in Condorrat. A full collection of his poems will be published by Smokestack Books in 2018.

Olga Wojtas writes from home in Edinburgh. She won a 2015 Scottish Book Trust New Writers Award.